CIRCULAR DORSET RAMBLES

BY

EDWARD GRIFFITHS

A SELECTION OF FAVOURITE CIRCULAR WALKS FOR AN
INTIMATE EXPLORATION OF
THE BEST OF DORSET

BY THE SAME AUTHOR

THE STOUR VALLEY PATH   ISBN 0 9519376 7 7

THE CRANBORNE CHASE PATH   ISBN 0 9519376 2 6

THE BLACKMORE VALE PATH   ISBN 0 9519376 3 4

RAMBLES FROM DORSET TOWNS   ISBN 0 9519376 5 0

HILL WALKING IN DORSET   ISBN 0 9530338 0 5

MORE CIRCULAR DORSET WALKS   ISBN 0 9530338 3 X

DEAD INTERESTING DORSET   ISBN 0 9519376 6 9

Clavell's Tower, Kimmeridge.   Page 82

First edition -1996 as 'Dorset in a Fortnight' ISBN 0 9519376 4 2
Re-published 1998 as 'Circular Dorset Rambles' ISBN 09530338 1 3
Fully revised edition published 2000

ISBN 0 9530338 4 8

Published by
Green Fields Books
13 Dalewood Avenue, Bear Cross
Bournemouth, BH11 9NR

CIRCULAR DORSET RAMBLES

CONTENTS

Cover picture: Ackling Dyke from Bottlebush Down with approaching storm

CIRCULAR DORSET RAMBLES

WALKS LOCATION MAP

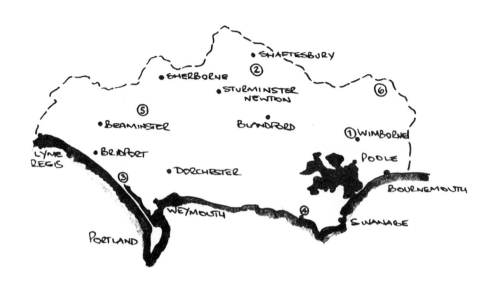

TITLE	WALKS	MILES
1. THE KINGSTON LACY CIRCLE	3	4.1/2 8 10.1/4
2. THE SPREADEAGLE SAUNTER	3	3.1/4 5.3.4 9
3. THE ABBOTSBURY AMBLE	2	4 8.1/4
4. THE ENCOMBE ENCOUNTER	3	5.1/4 6.3/4 8.3/4
5. THE MELBURY MEANDER	3	4.1/2 5.3/4 10.1/4
6. THE BOTTLEBUSH ROUND	4	5.1/4 5.1/4 7.1/2 12.3/4

CIRCULAR DORSET RAMBLES

INTRODUCTION

How this first book of circular walks in the series came about: Whilst researching for the first three Green Fields Books which were all long-distance trails, I was frequently tempted to wander from my selected routes and to amble, willy-nilly, about this most beautiful of counties (keeping to Rights of Way, of course). If you have walked either The Stour Valley Path, The Blackmore Vale Path or The Cranborne Chase Path, you will have experienced the same desire to find out where some of the adjacent Footpaths and Bridleways lead.

At the same time, I was asked many times by Dorset bookshops if I intended to produce any circular walks. I explained that I was trying to design long-distance routes for Dorset walkers in much the same way as the rest of Britain appears to be covered, criss-crossed with official long-distance Paths such as the Coast to Coast Walk, The Pennine Way (both by dear old A W Wainwright), Offa's Dyke Path, The Cotswold Way and The Dales Way.

However, I decided to complete this selection of circular walks - and, since then, a few more have followed (see list at front). The areas were specially chosen to reflect the diversity of landscape and the startling beauty of this wonderful county and, if you walk them all, you'll be exhausted but eager for more.

Here they are then. These Saunters, Meanders, Encounters or whatever are a miscellany of fine walks, some whole days and some half days, which begin and end at the same spot, in country, town or village where you can park a car or where local buses are available. All are within the normal range of a reasonably fit person who can live without a huge meal or a couple of pints in the middle of the day (but, before you set out, make sure I haven't given any dire warnings of steep hills which may cause you a problem). If you take just enough sandwiches and drinks to last until you get back - as well as the specified Ordnance Survey map, waterproofs and sun oil or extra jumpers (depending on which season you choose) - you'll be all set for a whole series of enjoyable and rewarding days out.

Each walk is completely different from any of its companions in this book. If one takes you over hills and vales or along coastal paths, the next may take you through farming land or along a river. One may take you to visit a small village or a market town whilst another may wander over chalk downs or along tracks and ancient roads. You won't be disappointed and, when you've tasted a few of these 'Delights of Dorset', you'll be counting the days to your next excursion.

The maps are highly detailed so you shouldn't have much trouble finding your way at any time but, if you happen to wander off the route, the relevant Ordnance Survey map which I recommend for each walk will soon bring you back.

Various bus companies serve the walking areas but the most used will be Wilts and Dorset, First Southern National and the smaller operators who are listed in 'Public Transport in Rural Dorset' which is obtainable from Tourist Information Centres throughout Dorset. These timetables, which give full addresses and telephone numbers of the operators, are also available from Environmental Services Directorate, Dorset County Council, County Hall, Dorchester, DT1 1XJ.

CIRCULAR WALKS IN THIS BOOK

Each walk begins with a description of the main features which you will meet during the day, together with the map reference for the start point, the Ordnance Survey map/s which you should carry, parking areas available and any buses which will take you there. There are mileage tables which will enable you to plan your journey and the highly detailed Stage maps show you how far you have come from the start. Follow the maps but don't miss the adjacent text because that is where you'll find the extra details that will add to your enjoyment of the walk. On a few occasions, I recommend that you stop walking to read the text but this is only when I'm concerned that you may walk over a cliff edge or miss a special view because your head is stuck in the book.

Wherever possible, I have tried to make a figure-of-eight configuration of walks from the chosen start or to offer a quick return alternative so that you can do a short circuit. Then, if you find that you aren't ready to go home yet, you can walk some more - and be sure that it'll be different from the walk you've just finished.

RIGHTS AND RESPONSIBILITIES

One point that is raised sometimes is, 'What if the way is blocked but there is an arrow pointing in a different direction?'.

Well, routes of Footpaths and Bridleways can be changed at the request of landowners, farmers or individuals for many different reasons. This is an ongoing state of affairs and changes can be made even as a new book is going into print. So, if you find a change which is accompanied by clear signs and/or waymarks, follow the changed route (usually only over a short distance) until it rejoins your route. However, if you should find a new, unsigned obstruction on the correct route, such as blocked or wired-up gates, stiles or exits from fields, you should make a reasonable deviation in order to continue on your route. Such obstructions are illegal under Section 137 of the Highways Act 1980 and any unauthorised blockages such as these should be reported to the Rights of Way Section at Dorset County Council, Dorchester - Telephone 01305-224463.

If you find a gate open, leave it open but, if it's closed, close it behind you - and don't drop litter. Observance of these two simple requests is all that is required to make the relationship between walker and farmer perfectly harmonious.

If you come across a ploughed field and the route crosses it or follows the edge of it, the Path or Bridleway has to be reinstated within 14 days of ploughing under the Rights of Way Act 1990. If these reinstatements have not been made, cross the field or follow the edge as you wish, whichever is easiest.

I know I don't really need to remind you but, as with all of the other books, I feel it behoves me to tell you that you will be visiting working areas of Dorset - not one gigantic theme park. Then again, if you find someone ploughing, harvesting, wood cutting, dry-stone wall building, foresting or sheep herding (I've seen all of these on these walks), they won't usually mind if you stop and watch for a while.

KEY TO MAP SYMBOLS

ROUTE	
FOOTPATH OR BRIDLEWAY ARROW	
SIGNPOST	
HEDGE	
WIRE FENCE	
WOOD FENCE/ IRON FENCE	
STONE WALL/BRICK WALL	
STILE	
GATE - LARGE / GATE - SMALL	
BRIDGE OVER STREAM	
TREE - DECIDUOUS / TREE - PINE	
SPECIFIC BUILDING	
GROUP OF BUILDINGS - SCHEMATIC	
STREAM/RIVER	
EMBANKMENT/HILLSIDE (arrows point down)	
TUMULUS/BARROW	
CLIFF EDGE	
OVERHEAD CABLES	
MILES FROM START OF WALK	
ADJOINING MAP NUMBER	

3

CIRCULAR DORSET RAMBLES

Top: Melbury Sampford. Page No 94

Bottom: St Mary's, Frome St Quintin. Page No 106

PART ONE - THE KINGSTON LACY CIRCLE

INTRODUCTION

With Wimborne Minster as base camp, two of these three walks include a short exploration of this popular market town, a relaxing and most pleasant stroll over the surrounding farmland and an inspiring visit to the Iron-age Badbury Rings hill fort with far-reaching views. If you have walked '*The Cranborne Chase Path*' you will be know some parts of the routes described here - but not as circular walks. Routes 1 and 2 both begin in Wimborne and the paths are easy to follow. The shorter Route 3 begins and ends at Badbury Rings. It uses some stages of Routes 1 and 2 with a connecting path along the B3082 beech avenue.

THE ALTERNATIVES

Routes 1 and 2 start outside the Minster Church of St Cuthburga (Ref. SZ009999 on O S Map No. 195). Route 3 starts in Badbury Rings car park on the B3082 between Wimborne and Blandford Forum (Ref. ST961032 on the same Map). The walks are between 4.1/4 and 10.1/4 miles, depending on which you choose.

ROUTE 1: Total distance 10.1/4 miles - This longest of the three Routes takes you through the centre of Wimborne, out on the Cranborne road and past Walford Mill. Field paths then take you past a fine Victorian waterworks en route to High Hall (a miniature Kingston Lacy) before following an easy country lane and farm tracks all the way to the 'Druid Oaks' of King Down Wood and to Badbury Rings. A stroll along the beech avenue of the B3082 brings you to a long, easy track which circumnavigates Kingston Lacy Park with fine views en route. After a tea stop at Pamphill, the River Stour Footpath provides the final leg into Wimborne.

ROUTE 2: Total distance 8.3/4 miles - This shorter route misses Badbury Rings so I would only recommend it if you would rather have a glimpse of the National Trust's medieval hunting lodge at Lodge Farm instead. Then again, you could do Route 1 and go back another time to walk Route 3 which also visits Lodge Farm.

ROUTE 3: Total distance 4.1/2 miles - This shortest of walks begins and ends in the car park at Badbury Rings and takes you on a stroll along the beech avenue on the B3082. It passes Lodge Farm before following undulating farm tracks and woodland paths back to Badbury Rings.

Damory Coaches 301, 302 and 320 pass Badbury Rings but you'll probably have to beg to be dropped off. So, unless you want to take your car there and have a shorter walk, the longer routes are better because you start and finish in Wimborne which has innumerable buses. These include: From Poole - Wilts and Dorset 132, 133, X32. From Bournemouth - Wilts and Dorset 132, 133. From Blandford and Shaftesbury - Wilts and Dorset 182, 183.

Once you've left Wimborne for the longer walks, you won't find any shops, tea-shops or pubs until you're nearly back again. So take a packed lunch and enjoy the walk, promising yourself a rewarding tea or some provisions from the Pamphill Dairy Farm Shop - or some sustenance at the Vine Inn on Stage 10. There are no shops at all on the shorter walk from Badbury Rings although you may find an ice cream van in the Car Park in high summer.

STAGE	MILES	TOTAL MILES
ROUTE 1:		
1 Wimborne Minster to Walford	.50	.50
2 Walford to Catley Copse	.75	1.25
3 Catley Copse to High Hall	.75	2
4 High Hall to Barnsley Lane	1	3
5 Barnsley Lane to Bradford Track	1.25	4.25
6 Bradford Track to Badbury Rings	1.25	5.50
7 Badbury Rings to Beech Avenue	.75	6.25
8 Beech Avenue to Kingston Lacy Drove	1.50	7.75
9 Kingston Lacy Drove to Pamphill	.75	8.50
10 Pamphill to River Stour	1.25	9.75
11 River Stour to Wimborne Minster	.50	**10.25**
ROUTE 2:		
To Barnsley Lane on Route 1 - Stages 1 to 4	3	3
5 Barnsley Lane to Chilbridge Junction	.50	3.50
5a Chilbridge Junction to Lodge Farm	1.25	4.75
8 Lodge Farm to Kingston Lacy Drove	.75	5.50
To Wimborne Minster on Route 1 - Stages 9 to 11	2.50	**8**
ROUTE 3		
7 Badbury Rings to Beech Avenue	.75	.75
8 Beech Avenue to Lodge Farm	.50	1.25
5a Lodge Farm to Chilbridge Tumuli	1	2.25
5 Chilbridge Tumuli to Bradford Track	1	3.25
6 Bradford Track to Badbury Rings	1	**4.25**

ROUTE LAYOUT

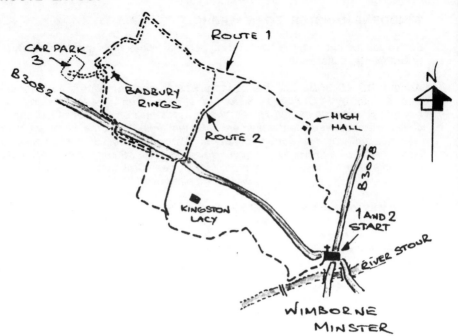

Kingston Lacy House. Page 26

STAGE 1

WIMBORNE MINSTER TO WALFORD

Before you set out from the North-facing porch of Wimborne's Minster Church of St Cuthburga, consider this:

Around 713 AD, a Benedictine nunnery was founded at what is now nearby Dean's Court by St Cuthburga, sister of Ina, King of the West Saxons and this Norman church with its mid-15thC West tower is built on the site of the abbey church which belonged to the nunnery. By that time, Wimborne was already an important settlement known as Wymburn or Winburnham because of its position on the banks of the River Wym where it joined the River Stour. In 871 AD, after the battle with the invading Danes at Martin, near Cranborne, King Alfred the Great buried his fatally wounded brother Ethelred here.

Above your left shoulder, you will see the Quarter Jack who was carved in 1613 and dressed as a monk. However, since the Napoleonic wars he has sported the livery of a Grenadier. He is connected to an entirely separate mechanism from the amazing astronomical clock inside the church and he has to be wound up every day.

You really should make a point of visiting this church to see the chained library, the Saxon chest, the Man in the Wall and the Uvedale monument - all as detailed in the Minster's 'Guide for Pilgrims and Visitors'.

Time to go now so, straight ahead, leave the churchyard and cross over Cooks Row, past the toilets and on across Cornmarket into Church Street. After the 'Oddfellow Arms', cross over West Street at the traffic lights with The Square on your right and The King's Head on your left. Continue along West Borough.

The Tivoli Cinema and theatre which you will soon pass on the left, was a fine 18thC house until its conversion into a cinema in the 1930s. It was abandoned in the 1970s and it lay neglected and unloved until restoration was begun in 1993 by the Tivoli Trust. It is once again a very popular venue.

After the traffic lights' junction, keep straight on past the Town Hall and School Lane on your left. Cross over to the right when your pavement runs out. Then, past Chapel Lane and the Stone Lane traffic lights, cross over East Borough to Walford Bridge where the River Allen flows. Opposite East Borough is Knobcrook Lane which leads to a fine 18thC flour mill which has been very successfully converted into the Walford Mill Craft Centre.

This mill warrants a return visit to view the constantly changing exhibitions by invited local artists, craftsmen and women together with the work of resident designers of textiles, ceramics, wood, jewellery, glass and metalwork. You could spend some very happy hours in Wimborne. There is a superb Market every Friday with smaller versions on Saturdays and Sundays. Visit the Tourist Information Centre in the High Street and they'll make sure you have a good time.

Now, cross over the bridge and continue out of Wimborne, passing 'The Crown and Anchor' Inn on the other side of the road and with a field on your right.

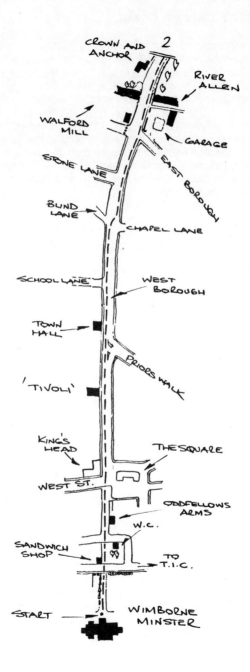

STAGE 2

WALFORD TO CATLEY COPSE

After Minster Garage on your left and before Shakespeare Road on your right, cross back over the main Cranborne road and turn onto the farm track which is signposted 'Public Footpath - High Hall'. Go through the kissing gate or cross the cattle grid very carefully and follow the track past two houses on your left with a wire-fenced, open field on your right.

After the barns on your left, the ground dips on the left to a hedge and some trees. This leads you to a stile and a farm gate as the track bears left. The right gates lead into the Wimborne Pumping Station and you will have a clearer view of the Victorian buildings in a few moments. The 'Footpath' arrow on the stile confirms that you should keep to this track and follow the right hedge between you and the Pumping Station.

Beyond the trees on your right, there is a high grass bank which probably forms a side of a water storage tank whilst, over on your left, a couple of wire fences show where the River Allen is flowing towards Walford Mill and Bridge.

Now, look back to the Pumping Station.   What a glorious, ivy-clad structure for what is purely a utility building.   Those Victorians certainly had style - like it or not - and they built things to last in those days.

As the track bears slightly round to the right, pass through the narrow, Footpath-arrowed opening by the side of the farm gate on your right and follow the right edge of the quite steep uphill field, past another opening into the right field, past a 'Keep Dogs on Leads' sign and past a cattle trough against the fence.   At the top right corner of this field, there is a conglomeration of signs and arrows ensuring that you keep to the right path.   There are yellow arrows on two posts, a large white arrow on the sign 'Keep Dogs on Leash' and a 'Private Woods - Keep Out' notice.   Do what you're told and turn left to follow the edge of Catley Copse (for so it is called) down the field to the gate in the hedge facing you at the bottom.   There is another Footpath arrow by the gate.

On your way down the field, you will see High Hall in the trees some way ahead of you and Badbury Rings and King Down Woods up on the horizon in the front left distance.   Badbury Rings is the high point with the thin woods on top.

Keep going, uphill now, past the right gate into the Copse, again signed 'Private Woods - Keep Out', until you reach the far end of the woods and the field opens out on your right.   Cross over the open field, aiming for High Hall in the distance and the electricity pylon ahead of you, a few fields away.   On the far side of your field, the track bearing right runs up to Wilksworth Caravan Park.   Go through the gate or squeeze through the Footpath-arrowed stile in the fence.   Here, a Footpath arrow points straight ahead on an indistinct path in the next field and you are instructed again to 'Keep Dogs on Leash'.   Cross the 180 yards wide field by aiming just left of the pylon (340º WNW).

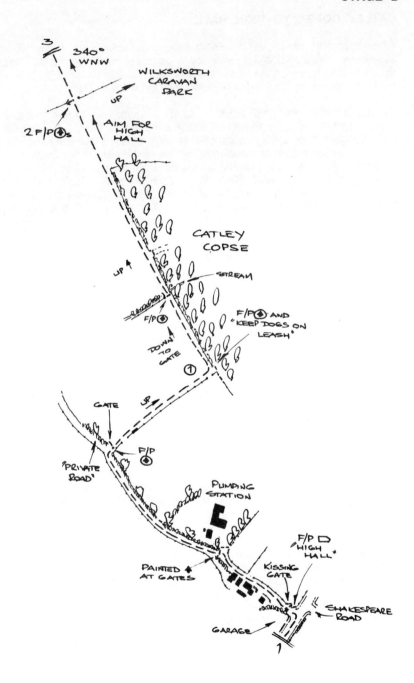

3

340°
WNW

WILKSWORTH
CARAVAN
PARK

UP

2 F/P⊕s

AIM FOR
HIGH
HALL

CATLEY
COPSE

UP

STREAM

F/P⊕

F/P⊕ AND
"KEEP DOGS ON
LEASH"

DOWN
TO
GATE

①

GATE   UP

F/P
⊕

"PRIVATE
ROAD"

PUMPING
STATION

F/P ☐
"HIGH
HALL"

PAINTED
AT GATES

KISSING
GATE

SHAKESPEARE
ROAD

GARAGE

1

11

STAGE 3

CATLEY COPSE TO HIGH HALL

Across this field, climb over the Footpath-arrowed stile into a narrow wood. A two-sleepers wide by 50 ft long walkway leads you through the wood. Climb over the stile in the fence on the other side and keep straight on for 200 yards, aiming to brush against the right leg of the electricity pylon in this field.

On the far side of the field, cross the faint track which straddles your path and climb over the stile in the fence and hedge into the next field. All of these stiles have Footpath arrows, so your direction is quite clear. Now, keep straight on up and over this high field to the stile to the left of the gate at the bottom. More Footpath arrows here and on the bridge across the River Allen, which is in the next field, point you towards High Hall. Over the bridge, look up the field and you will see the next stile in the far left corner (344º WNW) but don't aim straight for it. Veer left towards the wire fence and follow the fence to its end, going over a brick tunnel which carries the ditch water under your path. (The tunnel was breaking up on my latest visit, so it may have been repaired or replaced by now).

When the fence ends, keep straight on across the open field to the stile which leads into a strip of wood. This coppice is only 35 yards wide. Before leaving the Footpath-arrowed stile on the far side, look carefully up the next field and aim for the farm gate which stands just a little to the left up on the hill ahead of you, with a pair of fine oaks close to the top fence on the right. On your way up (at 350º WNW), you go past the edge of a small wood and, on your arrival at the gate, the two painted Footpath arrows confirm that you are still all right.

Go through the gate, remembering to close it behind you as there are usually some very smart ponies grazing in this field. *By the way, avoid eye contact with the ponies or they may become over-friendly. I have often found that ponies of this ilk have a penchant for leaning on human beings and, with the somewhat unfortunate weight differential, their affection can propel the inferior human earthwards at quite a rate.* Anyway, follow the perimeter hedge and fence of High Hall's garden and tennis court on your left. There is a Footpath arrow on the tennis court corner post.

On your way past, take a surreptitious look at the Hall, within the bounds of etiquette of course, and try to remember something of its style for later in the day when you'll have a glimpse of High Hall's bigger relation, Kingston Lacy - if you're staying on Route 1.

I'll tell you more about Kingston Lacy when you get there but, for now, a little potted history will suffice - *John Bankes had six daughters and a son, Ralph Bankes, who built Kingston Lacy. The youngest daughter, Arabella, married a Samuel Gilly and this gentleman built High Hall in about 1670 as a smaller version of Kingston Lacy which was completed only five years earlier. No doubt, his bride would have felt much at home here. By descent, High Hall passed to John Fitch who made his fortune in public works after the 1666 Great Fire of London. He passed his skills on to William, his son, who became a builder of equal repute and one of whose achievements was the construction of the South aisle of Wimborne Minster.*

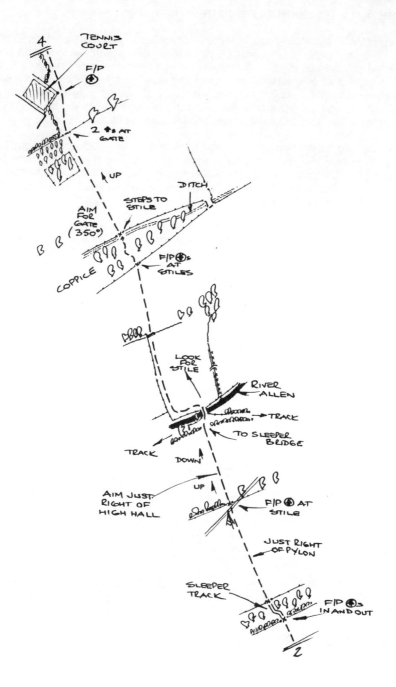

STAGE 4

HIGH HALL TO BARNSLEY LANE

Keep close to the fence, passing a gate which leads into the rear drive of High Hall, and then climb over the stile 65 yards along the left wire fence near to some gnarled and twisted oaks.   A Footpath arrow points towards the gates to the gravel drive.   Quietly walk towards them and leave High Hall by the small gate or over the cattle grid.   As you crossed the stile, a glance towards the house would have shown you a wood-clad water tower in the trees near to the house.   This tower looks something like the turret of a Bavarian castle.

Now, outside on the tarmac lane, with oaks and sweet chestnuts in High Hall's grounds behind you and with a farm track and a triplicity of gates opposite, turn left and begin a pleasant, easy walk along the lane with trees and hedges all around.   Because of the age of these trees, there is usually a variety of bird song accompanying this stroll.

Past a few gates into the fields to left and right and a track into the wood on your right, you arrive at a right bend in the lane which acquires a wide verge and a ditch on the left and a beech hedge alongside the wood on your right. Continuing up the lane, go past two cottages on your right and a few more gates in the hedges.

The next turning on the right, with the banked hedge just opposite a post box, is signed for 'Barnsley Farm'.   Don't turn off but prepare yourself for a long, slow uphill walk of about 3/4 mile along the straight lane.   With ditches and verges on both sides, go past Lower Barnsley Cottages, Barnsley House with its tennis court, past a small barn against the left hedge and the turning off to 'Lower Barnsley Farm', again on your left.   Keep on going with large fields on both sides.   Up on the horizon to your left is King Down Wood which is hiding Badbury Rings from your view.

High Hall from Barnsley Lane. This Page

14

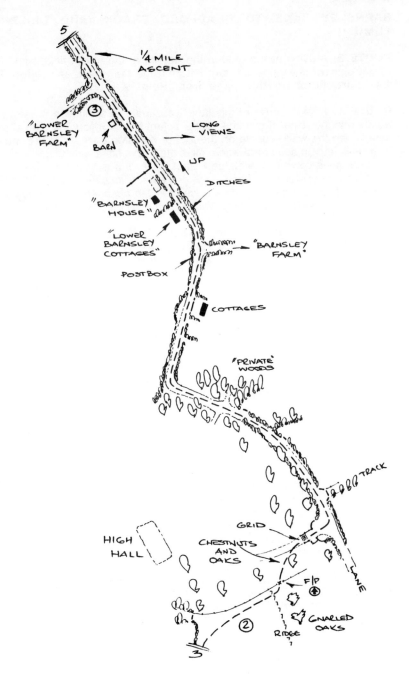

¼ MILE ASCENT

"LOWER BARNSLEY FARM"

③

BARN

LONG VIEWS

UP

DITCHES

"BARNSLEY HOUSE"

"LOWER BARNSLEY COTTAGES"

"BARNSLEY FARM"

POSTBOX

COTTAGES

"PRIVATE WOODS"

TRACK

GRID

CHESTNUTS AND OAKS

HIGH HALL

F/P

LANE

GNARLED OAKS

②

RIDGE

3

5

15

STAGE 5

BARNSLEY LANE TO BRADFORD TRACK (AND CHILBRIDGE TUMULI)

ROUTE 3: Arriving at the gate in the bottom of the tumuli field, with another B/Way-signed gate opposite, turn left onto the farm track and **follow Route 1's instructions on this page from Point X.**

ROUTE 1: After 1/2 mile of this lane, you arrive at a junction of farm tracks. Before this, however, if you look to the distant trees on your left, you should be able to see the white cupola on the roof of Kingston Lacy.   At the end of the lane, walk into an open area where all of the tracks have wide verges.   The first left track goes down to Chilbridge Farm.   *The farm is built close to an ancient crossing of the River Allen flood plains and derives its name from the Old English 'ceole' and 'bryeg' meaning the bridge over the channel.   It is a truly ancient establishment which belonged to Alcester Abbey in the Middle Ages.*

Whichever way you go from here, you cannot help but notice the great width of the farm tracks.   The next track goes to Lodge Farm and this is the turning for the shorter Route 2 which will deduct 2 miles from the day's walk.   But, now that you're here, it would be better not to miss Badbury Rings.   The extensive views from the top of this Iron age hill fort are much too spectacular to miss.

So, follow the main track straight on past an open silage area which is backed by a sparse hedge on your right.   After the open area, the track descends, narrower and stonier, between fenced fields, towards another distant junction.

In the field on your left, known as King Down, you will see two distinct tumuli, the first of many on this Route.   *In fact, the next stretch is alive with the memories of Iron age and Bronze age men and the Roman invaders who overtook their homes and their culture.*   Just keep on going down and you will arrive at opposing Bridleway-signed gates astride the track.

ROUTE 1 - POINT X: Keep straight on and you arrive at the junction where *'The Cranborne Chase Path'* turns right on its way to Salisbury.   For today, follow the zig-zag track straight ahead, past the small left copse and the facing right gate.   There is grass up the middle of the track as the stony track leads steeply uphill between the left hedge and the right fenced field.   On the way, you pass a pair of very wide gates and a stunted oak on the left and a gate into the right field. At the top of the track, after a collection of horse-jumps and with the track now enclosed by hedges, you begin a descent with good long views ahead and over on your right towards Manswood and Witchampton.

On the way down, go past the two gates which cross the track and the two gates into the side fields.   Levelling out, you arrive at a right turning with a house on the far corner and a Bridleway arrow on the near corner.   Keep straight on, past the hedged garden on your right and turn to Stage 6 - ignoring 5a on the next page.

ROUTE 2: If your mind is made up to cut 2 miles off your journey - turn left here and follow the Stage 5a map.

16

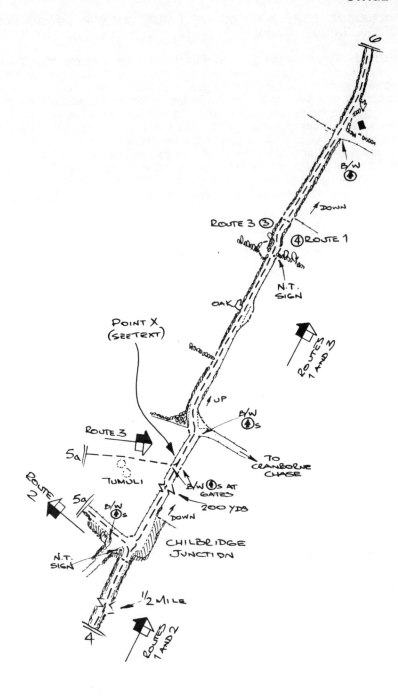

6

B/W ⑤

↑ DOWN

ROUTE 3 ③

④ ROUTE 1

N.T. SIGN

OAK

POINT X (SEE TEXT)

ROUTES 1 AND 3

↑ UP

B/W ⑤s

ROUTE 3

5a

TUMULI

TO CRANBORNE CHASE

B/W ⑤s AT GATES

200 YDS

ROUTE 2

5a

B/W ⑤s

↓ DOWN

N.T. SIGN

CHILBRIDGE JUNCTION

½ MILE

4

ROUTES 1 AND 2

17

CHILBRIDGE TUMULI TO LODGE FARM AND/OR LODGE FARM TO CHILBRIDGE TUMULI

ROUTE 2: Follow the straight, gravel track with a hedge on the left and a wire fenced field on your right.   Soon, the track bends left at a right gate with three Bridleway arrows.   Follow the track past a left gate at the bottom of the incline and back up to another gate in the left hedge just before a bend takes you round a fenced concrete enclosure which once housed a three-part barn. Immediately, you pass a wide, rough grassy area also on your left.   Here is a junction of tracks with a horse-jump in the wire fence facing you.   The track to the left leads to Chilbridge Farm whilst the right one leads to King Down Woods and Farm (both are private tracks).   Zig-zag left and right and join the continuing track with the hedge on the left side and another fenced field on the right.   Keep on, with slow ascents and descents, along the track.

At a small wood of old beech trees, you arrive at a gate and half a gate just before the B3082 Wimborne to Blandford road.   Emerging onto a wide verge with two Bridleway arrows, turn right and follow the green track parallel to the road with the fenced field on your right.   *On the other side of the road, you will see the fine, stone Kingston Lacy Lodge with a pair of stone pillars and wrought iron gates which lead onto a drive to Kingston Lacy House.   This drive was a continuation of the majestic avenue of beeches which runs for two miles ahead of you and past Badbury Rings but now the B3082 bends here and runs around the Eastern edge of Kingston Lacy Park and past the more modern, un-Lodged, entrance.*

Anyway, at the end of the right field, the drive on your right leads to the 14thC Lodge Farm.   Cross over the drive and continue along the wide verge track.

At about the time of the Peasants' Revolt, the present Lodge Farm house was a hunting lodge for the Manor of Kingston Lacy.   Apart from its superbly preserved architectural features inside, excavations have revealed many personal items which belonged to the 17thC occupants, the Short family.   These include many domestic items - and a mould which was used to forge shilling coins of William III. There are fascinating artefacts displayed here, including Neolithic, Bronze and Iron age items excavated nearby. .

Now turn directly to Stage 8.

ROUTE 3: Cross the Lodge Farm drive and turn next left at the Bridleway arrow post onto a long, gravel track.   *See text in italics above for information on Lodge Farm and Kingston Lacy Lodge.*   Follow the track for 1/2 mile and zig-zag across a four-way junction of tracks.   Keep straight on again until you reach a right bend with a 3-way Bridleway-arrowed gate on the left corner.   The left field Bridleway leads to two distinct tumuli, about 100 yards away at the top of the field.   Go through the gate and cross the field, keeping to the left of the tumuli. After the barrows, keep straight on along a descending path.

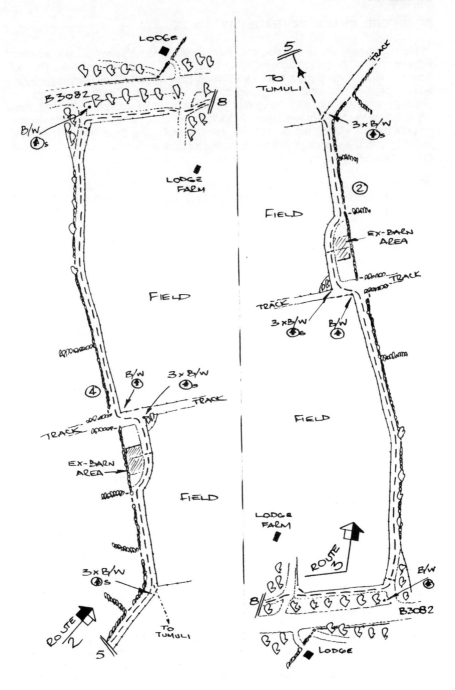

19

STAGE 6

BRADFORD TRACK TO BADBURY RINGS

At the left bend in the farm track, the wide grassy area on your right is where the Footpath from 'The Cranborne Chase Path' returns on the line of the Roman Ackling Dyke military road from Old Sarum (pre-Salisbury) to Badbury Rings, after 5 days of delightful wandering through Cranborne Chase. Ignore the Footpath-arrowed stile and the Bridleway arrow post facing you. Instead, turn left to follow the wide gravel track (Ackling Dyke) uphill with hedges and verges on both sides. At the top of the track, the line of Ackling Dyke goes straight on, invisibly, into the woods whilst the farm track takes an almost parallel line down to King Down Farm.

With two farm gates and a Bridleway arrow post on your left, turn right into the woods and follow the Bridleway's meanderings, never far from the wire fence of the field on your right.

In 'The Old Roads of Dorset', Ronald Good recalls that these old woods, called 'The Oaks' are 'of immense age, bowed and hollow, and festooned with lichens and ferns'. They are known locally as 'Druid Oaks' but this merely confirms their great age. In the early 16thC, that great traveller Leland visited "The famous wood of Bathan, near Badbury Rings'.

So, in the steps of the famous, follow the path through the tangled, mysterious wood. You eventually arrive at a junction of tracks with a Bridleway arrow post where you need to zig-zag left and right. Over the farm gate just a little right at this junction, you have your first view of the long beech avenue which runs along the B3082 to one of the Lodges of Kingston Lacy. Enjoying the last stretch of wooded Bridleway, you soon emerge on the far side of the wood onto a descending, fenced track.

On the way down, you will see Badbury Rings up on the left - suddenly very close after being hidden for so long. When the track reaches the bottom of the dip and has passed an overgrown shrubbery on your right, you arrive in a narrow thicket of trees and scrub. When you emerge onto the grassy slopes beyond, turn instantly left, uphill, between the dense scrub and a few hawthorns. Follow the edge of this 'Conservation Area' and cross the grassy track which comes from a gate over on your left.

Past a low tumulus on the right, keep straight on up the slope to a wooden gate in the fence which crosses your path. If you have a dog with you, the notice indicates that you will have to go around the perimeter fence of the Rings to join the main B3082 and turn left to meet the dog-less at the exit stile which is shown on your Stage 7 guide map. Everybody else, go through the gate (or walk down to the first kissing gate, if it's locked) and look for the Ordnance Survey trig point column on the inner ring over to your left.

Aiming generally for this column, head for a staircase up the slope of the outer ring. On the way, you cross over another track. This is the Ackling Dyke as it approaches the outer edge of Badbury Rings and continues past it to Maiden Castle - the bigger Roman-occupied hill fort just outside Dorchester (Durnovaria).

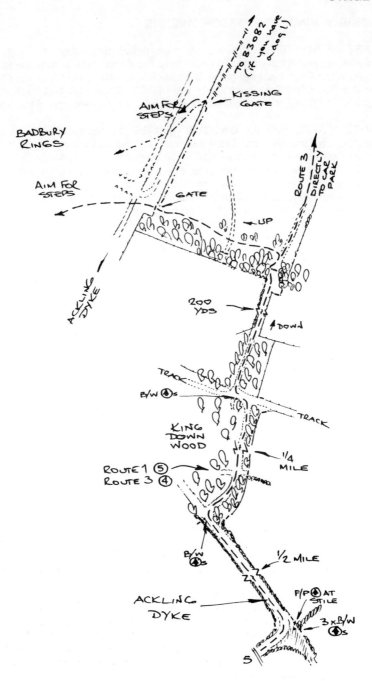

TO B3082
(if you have a dog!)

KISSING
GATE

AIM FOR
STEPS

BADBURY
RINGS

ROUTE 3
DIRECTLY
TO CAR
PARK

AIM FOR
STEPS

GATE

UP

ACKLING
DYKE

200
YDS

DOWN

TRACK

B/W ④s

TRACK

KING
DOWN
WOOD

¼
MILE

ROUTE 1 ⑤
ROUTE 3 ④

B/W
④s

½ MILE

ACKLING
DYKE

F/P④ AT
STILE

3 x B/W
④s

5

21

STAGE 7

BADBURY RINGS TO BEECH AVENUE

START OF ROUTE 3: From the car park, either go through the kissing gate and walk up to the top of the Rings or take the direct route across the long field parallel to the B3082 without going up to the Rings. Now, scan down to ROUTES 1 AND 3 TOGETHER and join Route 1 at PLINTH **'X'** on the top of Badbury Rings or at FIELD POINT **'Y'** on the far side of the field for the next part of the walk.

ROUTE 1 ARRIVING AT BADBURY RINGS: To reduce the erosion of this important site, the National Trust has built a series of inconspicuous steps into the embankments and I implore you to use them on your way to the O.S. column. The Stage map shows that the most direct route over the Rings actually leads you away from the O.S. column, towards the right, so go that way and double back towards the column when you reach the top of the inner ring.   Take your time to enjoy the views and to feel the magic of this historic site and, when you reach the column, rest awhile and I'll tell you something of the Rings.

Badbury Rings encloses an area of 14 acres whilst the central ring, with a depth of 40ft, measures 1 mile in circumference.   Built in the Stone age, it was occupied successively by Bronze age, Iron Age, Roman and Saxon settlers - all of whom would have been contained within high wooden palisades built upon the rings.   Named after Bada, the local chief of the Durotriges, Badbury Rings succumbed to the Roman invaders under Vespasian in the early days of the invasion of South-West England which began with the fall of the Isle of Wight (Vectis) in AD 45.   This camp was strategically placed on the main trading routes from (using the modern names) Poole, Dorchester, Exeter, Salisbury and onwards to London.

Now, turn back along the inner ring for a few yards and turn towards the centre, along the grass path between the old oaks.   Head up between the individual clusters of pines to the information plinth in the dead centre of the Rings.

ROUTES 1 AND 3 TOGETHER: Viewpoint **PLINTH 'X'** is aligned with its corners facing North, South, East and West.   When you have studied the map, leave the plinth and walk down the South avenue.   Having reached the top of the inner ring again, study the grassland down below you and you will see a definite grass track which leaves the Rings and runs to the avenue of trees along the main road.   Turn right for 50-60 yards along the top of the ring to find the best route out of the Rings, using steps where these are provided.   Follow that green track across open ground, filled with molehills and hawthorn bushes, until you reach the fence which encloses the Rings site.   The direct route for Route 3 comes across this field from the right and joins you here at **FIELD POINT 'Y'**.

The track ends at the fence but go over the stile about 10 yards to your right out onto a very wide verge between you and the ancient avenue of beeches along the Wimborne to Blandford road.   Turn left and follow the wide verge, past the right turn to Sturminster Marshall and past the car park area.   After the car park, keep on for a few more yards and, just past the T-junction sign over on the other side of the road, cross over to the equally wide right verge at the point with the longest, safest view of the traffic.

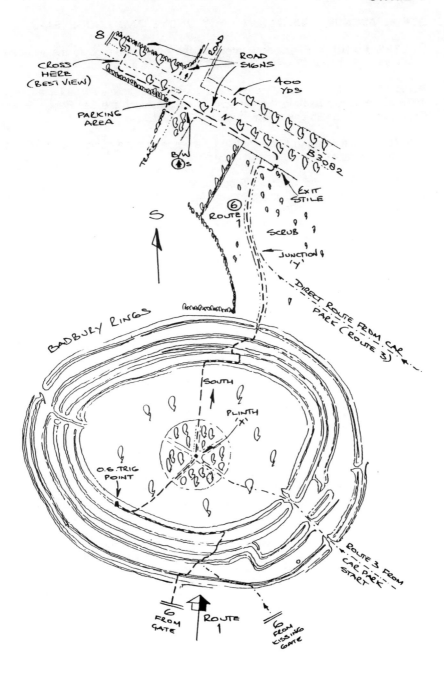

STAGE 8

BEECH AVENUE,   KINGSTON LACY DROVE AND LODGE FARM

ROUTES 1 AND 3: Everybody safely on the other side - go to the wooden gate in the right hedge 20 yards from the "200 yards to the Junction' sign.

ROUTE 3: Don't go through the gate but continue along this verge for another 1/4 mile and cross back to the left side when you reach the Car Park.   From there, turn to Stage 5a and follow the Route 3 instructions.

ROUTE 1: Go through the gate, leaving the verge and the traffic and entering a wide, grassy track between fenced open fields.

All of the land around Badbury Rings, Shapwick village, Kingston Lacy and almost into Wimborne itself was left to the National Trust in a massive bequest by the Bankes Estate in 1985 and also included the vast Bankes Estate lands around Corfe Castle in Purbeck.   Here, at Kingston Lacy, the 7000 acre estate includes the 250 acre wooded park around which you will be walking shortly .

Keep following this pleasant, grassy track between fenced hedges, slightly downhill to a zig-zag at the bottom.   After a dip around an older hawthorn hedge, the track begins to climb up again.   Now, steeply up and down, past an intruding piece of hedge on the way up, you walk past a replanted wood on your left at the top of the rise.   At the end of the track, a wired opening leads into the field on your right where one large and one small gate lead you onto an ancient Bridleway known as Sweetbriar Drove.   A 3-way Bridleway post points along all of the tracks.   Turn left.   The hedge which is now on your right contains many beech, oak and ash trees but some of these have these have been felled recently and supplemented by replanted specimens in wood frames.

Over this hedge, you can look down into the beautiful Stour Valley.   Keep following Sweetbriar Drove, past many gates, openings and 'Private' tracks, to a T-junction at its end.   With a 3-way Bridleway arrow post, near to a 'Private' gate which leads into Kingston Lacy Park, turn right.

ROUTE 2: Cross over the B3082 into the wide track which runs past the Car Park for visitors to Lodge Farm.   After nearly half a mile of pleasant wandering along this track with Kingston Lacy Park on your left and fields on your right, you meet Route 1 coming from the right at a T-junction with a Bridleway arrow post.

ROUTES 1 AND 2 TOGETHER: Trying to get a glimpse of Kingston Lacy House through the trees on your left, follow the grass and gravel track, passing an overhanging beech tree on the way.   At the next left bend, another wide green track goes off to the right.   This is the turning taken by 'The Stour Valley Way' and it is signed for 'Sturminster Marshall'.   Just keep following the main track around the Park, signed for 'Pamphill'.

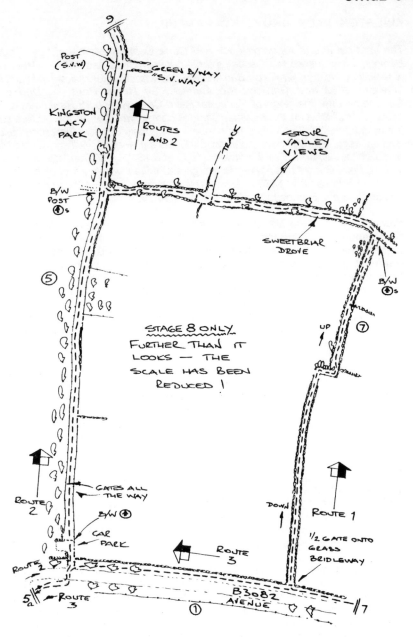

9

POST
(S.V.W)

GREEN B/WAY
"S.V. WAY"

KINGSTON
LACY
PARK

ROUTES
1 AND 2

TRACK

STOUR
VALLEY
VIEWS

B/W
POST
⊕s

SWEETBRIAR
DROVE

B/W
⊕s

⑤

STAGE 8 ONLY
FURTHER THAN IT
LOOKS — THE
SCALE HAS BEEN
REDUCED !

UP

⑦

ROUTE
2

GATES ALL
THE WAY

DOWN

ROUTE 1

B/W ⊕

CAR
PARK

ROUTE
2

ROUTE
3

½ GATE ONTO
GRASS
BRIDLEWAY

B3082
AVENUE

①

5
a

ROUTE
3

7

25

KINGSTON LACY DROVE TO PAMPHILL

The vast estates of Kingston Lacy and Corfe Castle were bought by Sir John Bankes, Chief Justice in Charles I's time, between 1632 and 1635.   The house was built by his son, Sir Ralph Bankes (the one whose sister resided in High Hall), between 1663 and 1665 by the architect Sir Roger Pratt.   During the Commonwealth (the reign of Parliament and Cromwell), both Bankes and Pratt spent a lot of time on the continent, out of harms way, but, at the restoration of the monarchy, Sir Ralph built this house.   Originally of brick, the entire building was encased with Chilmark stone for Sir Ralph's grandson, William, by his friend and architect, Charles Barry, between 1835 and 1840.   William later went to live in Italy, from where he sent marble fittings and Italian woodwork back to Kingston Lacy, until his death in 1855.   It was William's grandson, Sir Ralph Bankes, who bequeathed the Estates to the National Trust in 1985.

Now, after that potted history and making a mental note to come and enjoy the house and grounds another day, keep following the track for another 1/2 mile, past several 'Private' gates into the woods on your left and with hedged fields on your right.   A ditch appears first on your left and later on your right.   Just after two openings into the right fields, there is an estate cottage on your left which has a small but beautifully kept garden.   Just after the cottage and the 'Strictly Private' gate after it, you arrive at the 'South Lodge Car Park' with an access barrier across your track.   You will find another 'Stour Valley Way. Pamphill' sign on the corner and, although you are going to Pamphill, *don't* follow the signed direction down to the right with the pines on the roadside bank.

Keep straight on up Abbot Street, the lane with the ornately-gated gardens on the right where produce for the 'big house' was grown.   Walk past the greenhouses and onwards, next passing two more cottages dated 1907 and the field beyond them.   All this time, the encircling woods are still over on your left.   On the next bend, a gate opens onto a farm track which leads up to the red-brick outbuildings and barns of Manor Farm whilst another gated track leads down to the National Trust wood yard in the trees on your left.

You are still skirting around 'Manor Farm'.   On the bend in the road, the next two gates lead onto drives to Manor Farm's outbuildings and the lane then begins to ascend between higher banks.   There is a cottage either side of the left turning, high up on hedged banks, whilst there are some fine old oaks in the field up on your right.   The first cottage stands on the line of the Roman road from Badbury Rings which crosses your path here.

At the top of this gully, the old red-brick blacksmith's forge stands squarely against the roadside on your right.   This is closely followed by 'Forge Cottage' and another hedged cottage with a thatched summer house on the corner.   If you had followed the Stour Valley Way sign from the car park down the lane, you would have been returning to our route up the track past this summer house. This is All Fools Lane and it leads down to Cowgrove - away from our present route.   You can see where walkers on the Stour Valley Way have cut across the verge to go down All Fools Lane.   Now, keep straight on up the lane for a few more yards, still with the woods on your left and a field hedge on your right.

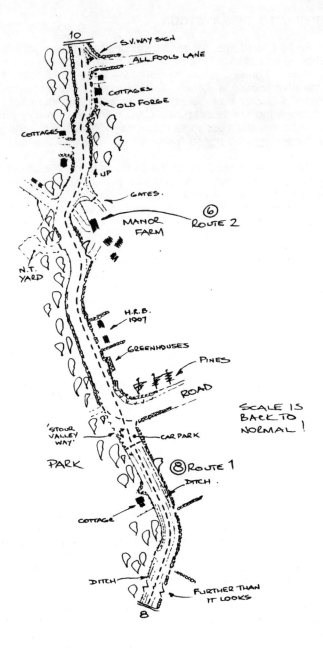

10

S.V. WAY SIGN

ALL FOOLS LANE

COTTAGES
OLD FORGE

COTTAGES

4 UP

GATES.

⑥ ROUTE 2

MANOR
FARM

N.T.
YARD

H.R.B.
1907

GREENHOUSES

PINES

ROAD

SCALE IS
BACK TO
NORMAL !

'STOUR
VALLEY
WAY'

CAR PARK

PARK

⑧ ROUTE 1

DITCH .

COTTAGE

DITCH

FURTHER THAN
IT LOOKS

8

STAGE 10

PAMPHILL TO RIVER STOUR

Just past All Fools Lane, the road continues around a slight left bend, passing the white gated entrance to St Stephen's Church on its way to the Pamphill Dairy Farm Shop. *You can get a nice cup of tea in the Tea Rooms there or a snack from the Shop to bring away with you if you would like to rest awhile on a bench by the Pamphill Cricket Pitch.* Either now or when you return from the Shop, turn right through the low wooden posts and follow the straggly path through the trees. Cross a small ditch with the railway-sleeper bridge and you will be in a gravel car parking area signed 'National Trust - Pamphill Green.

This village green dates back to the 13thC and was the site of the fairs which were granted to the lords of Kingston Lacy. The superb avenue of oaks was planted in 1846 and it leads straight to St Stephen's Church. However, the church wasn't built until 1907, the same year as the two cottages which you passed on the right after South Lodge Car Park. It is in the late decorated style, by C E Ponting, and its details are influenced a great deal by the Arts and Crafts movement of that period. Over on your left there is a collection of farm cottages including the rather unusual 18thC, thatched Pamphill Farmhouse with its ornamental caps on the chimneys and with an added, castellated porch. Beyond the car park, behind the hedge at the end of an elevated track, lies the superb late 17thC Pamphill Manor House. This was built by Matthew Beethall, steward to Sir Ralph Bankes, and a fine stable block was added to the right of the house in the 18thC.

Now, carry on along the grass to the right of the Oak Avenue and, when you arrive at the edge of the cricket pitch, you will find a bench beneath the old oak tree, facing the thatched 1909 cricket pavilion. *Late on a summer evening, there probably isn't a better place to be in all England, with a village cricket match drawing to its close - especially if you have a little something from the Farm Shop to nibble.*

At the end of the avenue, go past the anti-car barriers and an array of gates on the right and follow the road past Pamphill Village School. *This was built in 1698 by Roger Gillingham as a school and almshouse.* After a lane comes in from the right, skirting Pamphill Common, keep straight on. Before the first cottage on Vine Hill, turn sharp left and cross the grassy area to an electricity pylon. Directly underneath the pylon, bear right by the 3-way Footpath signpost and drop down some steps between bushes to the first of several squeeze-stiles. Through the stile, follow the path down to the left, with an embankment on your right and a few trees, a ditch and a fenced field on your left. More steps bring you to a junction of paths and, ignoring all others, take the right Footpath, along a row of trees and with the parallel bank up on your right.

A stream runs down on your left and, after the next stile, you cross open ground with a wooden fence on your right to cross over this stream with a plank bridge and another stile. Turn right at the Stour Valley Way signpost and follow the edge of the stream through this field. Over the stile at the end of the field, turn right onto the Cowgrove road, then go over the next stile in the left hedge, opposite Vine Hill, into the field with a hedge and ditch on your left.

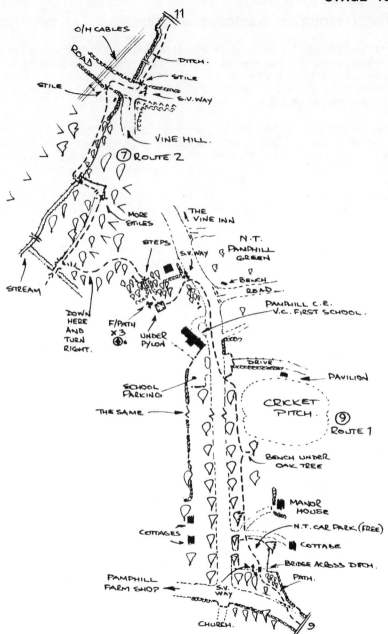

11

O/H CABLES

ROAD

DITCH.

STILE

STILE

S.V. WAY

VINE HILL.

⑦ ROUTE 2

MORE STILES

THE VINE INN

N.T. PAMPHILL GREEN

STEPS

S.V. WAY

BENCH

ROAD

PAMPHILL C.E. V.C. FIRST SCHOOL.

STREAM

DOWN HERE AND TURN RIGHT.

F/PATH ×3 ④

UNDER PYLON

SCHOOL PARKING

THE SAME

DRIVE

PAVILION

CRICKET PITCH.

⑨ ROUTE 1

BENCH UNDER OAK TREE

MANOR HOUSE

N.T. CAR PARK (FREE)

COTTAGE

COTTAGES

BRIDGE ACROSS DITCH.

PATH.

PAMPHILL FARM SHOP?

S.V. WAY

CHURCH.

9

STAGE 11

RIVER STOUR TO WIMBORNE MINSTER

Heading towards the River, cross over the stream on the left, using the signed footbridge and the squeeze-stile.   In this next field, keep following the wide grass path to the next stile with another bridge across a ditch.   On the bank of the River Stour, there is a magnificent willow tree with long branches gracefully hanging from its vast bulk.

Keep straight on, ignoring another path which bears off to your left, and follow the short fence to the corner of the facing hedge, beyond which a singularly unused stile stands at the end of a broken wire fence.   With the fence on your left, and with football pitches on the other side, keep following the river, past a surface water outfall.   After a few small trees, you emerge into some allotments with a track coming from your left.   Aim for the Minster Church which you will see directly ahead of you and don't turn off the track at all.   At its end, a Footpath sign points back to Eye Bridge which is just a little upstream from where you joined the Riverside path.   *Eye Bridge stands next to an ancient, and still used, ford crossing which is close to the point where the Roman road from Badbury Rings crossed the Stour on its way to Moriconium (now Hamworthy, Poole).*

When you leave the allotments and join a tarmac road with a block of flats on your right, follow the road around to the left, between townhouses and garages, past the Pay and Display car park on the left and the small factory unit on the right. In a few yards, you reach the B3082 Wimborne to Blandford Road where it is still called Victoria Road.   There is another Pay and Display car park on the corner of Old Road as you leave it.

Now, be very careful!   Wimborne is usually very busy and you've been away from the hurly-burly of everyday life for most of today.

Cross Victoria Road and turn up West Street, past the 'Pudding and Pye' on Pye Corner, past a garage and a few small shops and houses along the road.   Where the road bends around to the left, turn into the lane on your right.   Just ahead is the old Wesleyan Chapel and, bending left and right, you arrive in Cornmarket. In this pedestrianised area, close to the 'White Hart Inn', there are plenty of benches - but you're nearly there now.   So stroll into Cooks Row and turn onto the Minster path where the glass porch doors are waiting to welcome you back after a lovely day's rambling.

Don't forget to come back again to Wimborne Minster and Kingston Lacy.   You'll have a great day or two amidst the grandeur of Kingston Lacy and its Park and around the fine, historic town of Wimborne Minster.   There's plenty to see.

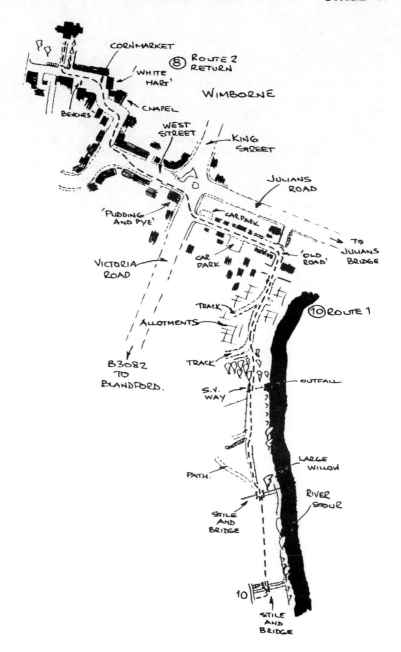

PART TWO - THE SPREADEAGLE SAUNTER

INTRODUCTION

With the buzz of single-engined aeroplanes, the twittering of skylarks and the constant bleating of sheep, the car park of Spreadeagle Hill, which stands on the airy downs of the Western end of Cranborne Chase and overlooks the Eastern edge of the Blackmore Vale, has long been a favourite spot for starting breezy walks or as a superb viewpoint above the River Stour plains for the less mobile.

Unfortunately, only one 401 bus a week ventures near to Spreadeagle Hill and Ashmore so we will use the car park (Reference ST886187 on O S Map No. 183) as our base for exploring the villages of East Compton and Compton Abbas (Nestling between Compton and Fontmell Downs) on Routes 1 and 3 and Ashmore (the highest village on Cranborne Chase with its Neolithic dew pond) on Routes 2 and 3, . The downs, forests and valleys which separate these villages from each other are filled with birds, rabbits, deer, sheep, cows - and ghosts. Well, that's not strictly true because the ghosts have, apparently, been laid - but more of that later.

As with most of the other walks in this book, I have tried to introduce alternative Routes which will help you to plan long or short walks or to change your mind on the way round.

THE ALTERNATIVES

By using the car park as the mid-point of the longest walk, you can descend almost instantly to the Compton villages and amble back up Fontmell Down. Then, on your return, you can decide whether to continue to Ashmore, Washers Pit and Fontmell Wood or to return another day for that entirely different walk.

ROUTE 1: Total distance 3.1/4 miles - This Route uses grassy paths and chalk tracks over high, breezy Compton Down and takes you down to join country lanes around the villages and churches of the Comptons. One church has been abandoned but the other, St Mary's in Compton Abbas, is well worth a visit. If you're there at the right time, you can get a cream tea in Compton Abbas - and that is your only chance to buy refreshment on any part of the 'Spreadeagle Saunter'. Your return is by more grassy paths up and along Fontmell Down.

ROUTE 2: Total distance 5.3/4 miles - This Route takes you away from the escarpment of Cranborne Chase and shows you more of the hinterland with its ancient woods and deep valleys. Within the first few yards, you find yourself on top of Melbury Down, preparing to cross the air-strip of Compton Abbas Airfield. From there, you join a forest track through West Wood and, after descending to Shepherds' Bottom, you walk up to Ashmore. After a short exploration of the village, you follow tracks to Washers Pit with its spooky goings-on. More woodland paths - just when you're feeling a little scared - lead you back, through Fontmell Wood, to cross the top road and return along a high National Trust path.

ROUTE 3: Total distance 9 miles - This is a combination of Routes 1 and 2 but it gives you a wonderful whole day's walking with the chance to enjoy and compare the completely different landscapes offered by both Routes.

STAGE	MILES	TOTAL MILES
ROUTE 1:		
1 Spreadeagle Hill to East Compton	1.25	1.25
2 East Compton to Compton Abbas	.75	2
3 Compton Abbas to Spreadeagle Hill	1.25	**3.25**
ROUTE 2:		
1 Spreadeagle Hill to West Wood	1.25	1.25
2 West Wood to Ashmore	1	2.25
3 Ashmore to Washers Pit	1.75	4
4 Washers Pit to Fontmell Fields	.75	4.75
5 Fontmell Fields to Spreadeagle Hill	1	**5.75**
ROUTE 3:		
Route 1 Stages 1 - 3 plus Route 2 Stages 1 - 5		**9**

ROUTE LAYOUT

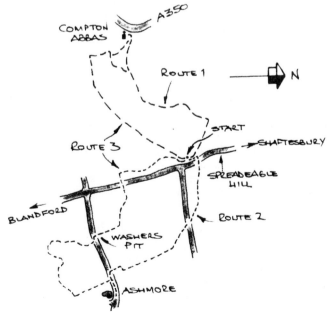

SPREADEAGLE HILL TO EAST COMPTON   OR TO WEST WOOD

On arrival at the gravel parking area at the top of Spreadeagle Hill, have a long look down into the plains of the River Stour.   This is a fine viewpoint at just under 750 ft above sea level and, on a clear day, you can see Hambledon Hill fort down on your left and, sweeping across the plain, Sturminster Newton and Sherborne.

Walk out of the car park and turn left along the edge of the road for 280 yards. You should walk on top of the left verge or face the traffic by walking on the right side of the road.

ROUTE 1 TO EAST COMPTON: When you reach a farm track on your left, go over the stile onto Compton Down with a fence on your left and a N.T. 'Melbury Hill' sign on the right.   Follow the long fence - noticing a gate over the fence from whence emerges a farm track - until you come to a half-gate.   Ancient cross dykes lie just to your right.   Go through the gate and walk away from the fence, over the saddle between Compton Down and Melbury Hill.   Melbury Beacon is over on your right, at 863 ft.   Over the brow you will find the farm track which comes from the gate that you noticed earlier.   Join this track and follow it downhill to a gate next to another N.T. 'Melbury Hill' sign.   Go through the gate into a sloping field and follow the track down to the farm gate in the bottom left corner.   Through this gate, keep on the track, alongside the right fence and past a gate, to a final gate which leads onto a muddy track with farm buildings and two gates on your left and a high bank on your right.   Follow the track down to a T-junction with a tarmac lane and turn left.   Now turn to Route 1 - Stage 2.

ROUTE 2 TO WEST WOOD (FOR ASHMORE): 20 yards before a farm track on the left, cross over the road and go through the Footpath-arrowed gateway into a high field.   The path along the right hedge is very long and much abbreviated on the Stage Map so take your time and enjoy the views into the valley over on your left.   After nearly 1/2 mile (slightly less distance after the wind-sock than before it), climb up onto a pair of stiles onto the airfield.   From this vantage point, look across the landing strip to the wood on the far side.

The very long wood is darkest where dense pines are growing.   At its left end, you can see where a couple of old oaks let in more light.   The arrowed Footpath heads diagonally (104º E) across the landing strip and the wide areas before and after it.   The official Footpath aims for those open oaks on the far left end because it still follows the ancient route between Melbury Abbas and Ashmore and, although you can't see it any more on this side, you will be walking on it along the far edge of the opposite woods.   Now, walk quickly and carefully across, maintaining your direction and looking left and right for approaching aircraft as you progress.

Breathless but safe, you will arrive at a stile, about 20 yards right of a gate, in a wooden fence.   Over the stile, cross the narrow field at the same angle, diagonally left, to a stile in the roadside hedge and cross the road into 'West Wood'.   Go around the barrier onto the track which descends slightly with a row of trees, a wire fence and a field on your left and with the deep woods on your right.   Keep following the long track down and turn directly to Route 2 - Stage 2.

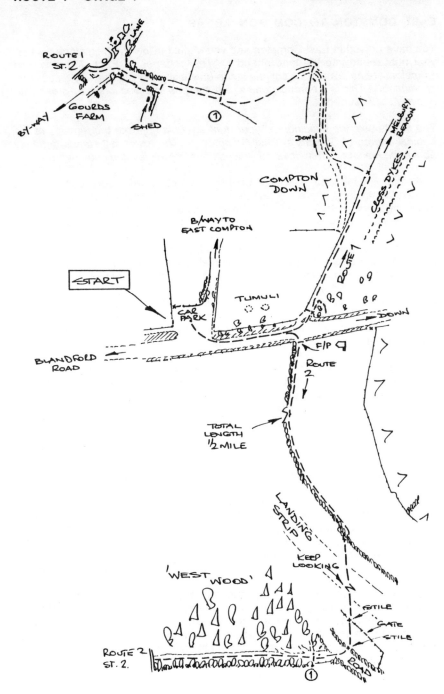

EAST COMPTON TO COMPTON ABBAS

You have arrived in East Compton and you should follow the high stone wall on your right round into the lane ahead.   *The cottages of East Compton and Compton Abbas are almost entirely stone-built using the Shaftesbury glaucanitic sandstone.   This is a porous stone which matures to a pleasant grey-green with a lovely rustic surface .*

The farmhouse and buildings on your right are built opposite the remains of the original church of St Mary's, East Compton.   The tower still stands defiantly above the leaning, lichen-covered gravestones in the elevated churchyard .

Keep following the lane, passing a Bridleway turning down to your left.   After a left bend in the lane, there is a bungalow and a row of cottages with a telephone box in the verge, followed by 'Lot's Cottage' - all on your left.   The right hedge is on a high bank as the lane drops to a left turning by a long, stone corner house.

At this T-junction, keep straight on to visit St Mary's church in Compton Abbas or turn left for the quickest way back to Fontmell Down.   It's only 200 yards to the church and it's not much out of the way so I'll assume that you're all going straight on.   Uphill now, with banked hedges either side, keep going until you pass the old chapel on your left and a fine stone cottage on the next left corner. The long stone cottage on the opposite right corner is 'The Old Forge'.   Go past the left turning for now, and go up the steps in the left embankment into a small wood which adjoins the very busy A350 road from Shaftesbury to Blandford.

Follow the path through the woods and down a single step onto the lawn of the Compton Abbas School, past a bench and the swings.   Quietly pass the school building and keep close to the iron fence on your way to the steps and gate which lead you into the barrier-protected area next to the A350.   There is another bench, commemorating the Coronation of Queen Elizabeth 2nd, in this stone wall so you may be permitted a short break.   There are bus stops for Shaftesbury and Blandford here, also a telephone box and a post box so communication with the outside world is relatively easy from here.   If you feel like a cream tea, there is a Tea Room just down the road towards Blandford - but mind the traffic.

Compton, meaning 'farm in the valley', comes from 'cumb' and 'tun'.   In 955 AD, a Charter granted 10 hides of land in Compton to the Nunnery at Shaftesbury; hence the Abbas connection.   The first church, of indeterminate date, was pulled down and some of the stones were used in the foundations of this 1867 church of St Mary.   It has a Norman font and a chalice of 1665 - the 'Cumpton Abbies Cup' so it clearly has a history.   It's a pity there are no guides available.

Now, back outside, return through the school grounds and out into the lane opposite The Old Forge (B & B at the time of writing).   Turn right at the foot of the steps and right again to descend the high-banked, tree and harts tongue fern-filled lane to emerge at the bottom where those who aren't visiting the church will come down the lane from your left.   Turn right and follow the lane, past 'Old Dairy Farm' cottage.

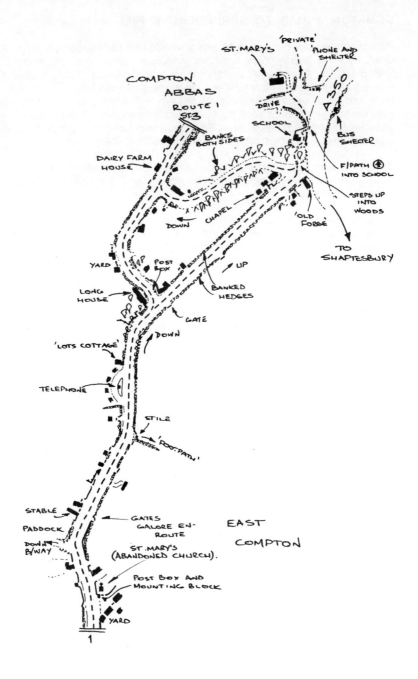

ST. MARY'S

'PRIVATE'

PHONE AND SHELTER

COMPTON ABBAS

ROUTE 1 ST.3

DRIVE

SCHOOL

350

BANKS BOTH SIDES

BUS SHELTER

DAIRY FARM HOUSE

F/PATH INTO SCHOOL

STEPS UP INTO WOODS

CHAPEL

DOWN

'OLD FORGE'

TO SHAPTESBURY

YARD

POST BOX

UP

LONG HOUSE

BANKED HEDGES

GATE

DOWN

'LOTS COTTAGE'

TELEPHONE

STILE

'FOOT PATH'

STABLE

PADDOCK

DOWN B/WAY

GATES GALORE EN-ROUTE

ST. MARY'S (ABANDONED CHURCH).

EAST

COMPTON

POST BOX AND MOUNTING BLOCK

YARD

1

ROUTE 1 - STAGE 3

COMPTON ABBAS TO SPREADEAGLE HILL

With the high bank on your right and a wooden fenced garden on your left, turn down into the grassy track with the overgrown stone wall, signposted 'Gore Clump 1.1/2'.   After the left paddock there is a pond which feeds a small stream running alongside this path before it disappears on your left.   There is an open bank and some trees leading around the right/left zig-zag as you pass a garden gate and a field gate on your right.   Upwards now, keep following this sunken, shady path with high fields on either side, around another right bend and down again to a half gate which brings you out into a long, downhill field.

Follow the wire fence on your right, down past a farm gate and a circular cattle trough, from where your narrow path continues uphill, past a small, banked clump of trees on your right.

Go over the unsigned stile by the next farm gate which faces you and swing round to your left, keeping close to the fences if the ground is ploughed or cropped.   Aim for the green track which goes up between the banked trees and the right wire fence to a gate with an adjacent white arrow.

Through the gate, you will see another National Trust sign telling you that you are on the lower slopes of Fontmell Down.   Sheep and cattle tracks come in from your right and cross the slopes whilst your track leads steeply uphill past a few hawthorns and, narrowing, goes by a slumped, chalky area on the right.   The slopes drop away quite steeply to your left but this track is a fairly comfortable climb.   When you reach the right wire fence near the top of the incline, go past the N T-arrowed stile to Fore Top and keep following the grassy track.   After the mixed wood on your right, go past another Footpath-arrowed stile and cross another dyke similar to that on Compton Down.   Now, follow the right wire fence all the way to the N T-signed stile next to the farm gate which opens onto your starting point.

If you're only doing the shorter Route 1 today, you've arrived - but, if you're going to complete the **Route 3** 'total' circuit, turn back to Stage 1 and follow **Route 2** directions for Compton Abbas Airfield and West Wood.   This fine walk covers a fascinating 5.3/4 miles, so you shouldn't miss it.

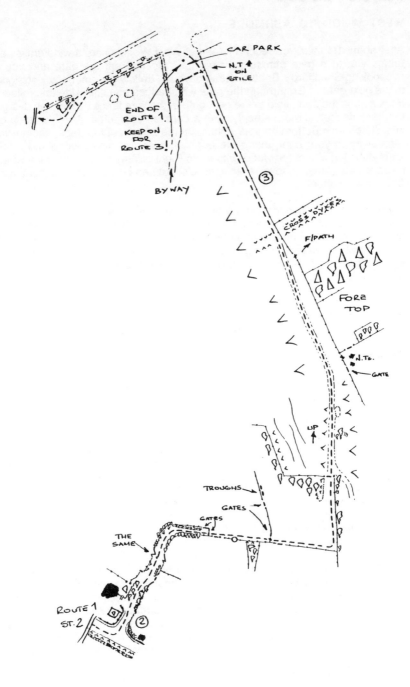

CAR PARK

N.T
ON
STILE

END OF
ROUTE 1.

KEEP ON
FOR
ROUTE 3!

BY WAY

③

CROSS DYKE

F/PATH

FORE
TOP

N.Ts.

GATE

UP

TROUGHS

GATES

GATES

THE
SAME

ROUTE 1
ST. 2

②

WEST WOOD TO ASHMORE

After about 1/4 mile, you reach the end of West Wood where a wide grassy area brings you to a gate across your path.   Go through the gate and you are overlooking Shepherd's Bottom ahead of you.   Follow the green track straight on to the next gate.   Go through the gate with hedges on either side and follow the track across the open field to the next gate in the wire fence.   Through this gate, the track descends more steeply, with a bank on your left and with a steep drop into Shepherd's Bottom on your right.   At the bottom of the track, another track runs away to your right, along the edge of a strip of mixed woodland.   Skirt around the left end of the wood, with a 'No Right of Way' gate on your left where a pre-enclosure map shows a shepherd's hut, and begin your ascent out of Shepherds Bottom.

Through the farm gate, follow the grassy track up to the next fence with a wire fence on your left and a steep bank on your right.   Still climbing, the track fades as you approach the next gate and the field is frequently full of deep cow-prints in the soft soil.   Before the top gate, bear right and follow the hedge along a row of ivy-clad trees.   In about 100 yards, go through the left Bridleway-signed gate onto a wide, fence-enclosed track between two fields.

Caution: If the track is overgrown with nettles in high summer, you will have little choice other then to return to the top gate and find your way through Manor Farm's cattle yard to the Ashmore road - explaining to the farmer on your way.

On arrival at the road, turn left for Ashmore.   The road down to your right leads straight to Washers Pit - but don't be in too much of a hurry to get there. Ashmore is well worth a visit and there's a lovely, easy stroll off the road and through some special ancient woods if you come with me.   So, follow the stone wall-lined road towards Ashmore, past the entrance to Manor Farmhouse on your left, and we'll go into the village first.

Ashmore, from 'aesc' and 'mere' meaning 'pool where ash-trees grow', is the highest village on Cranborne Chase.   Listed as Aisemare in the Domesday Book, Ashmore's stone and flint Church of St Nicholas was built in 1423, repaired in 1692 and completely rebuilt in 1874 by Charles Edwards - destroying the best of the old church in the process.   (Incidentally, two of the churchwardens at that date were George Rabbetts and George Hare).   The cottages and houses along the road are built from a variety of brick, flint and the local greensand stone and roofed with clay tiles or thatch.

The Neolithic dew pond is just around the corner, after the 1855 Methodist Chapel and the Old Parsonage.   In much simplified terms, it works by initial condensation of mist upon the specially constructed, insulated surface and thereafter by attracting moisture to the water surface, which is cooler than the surrounding atmosphere, faster than it can evaporate.   For details on how to construct one, see 'The Cranborne Chase Path'.   It didn't dry out during the drought of 1976 and had to be drained in 1994 so that it could be resealed.

Now turn to Stage 3 for the Bridleway that you passed on the right on the way in.

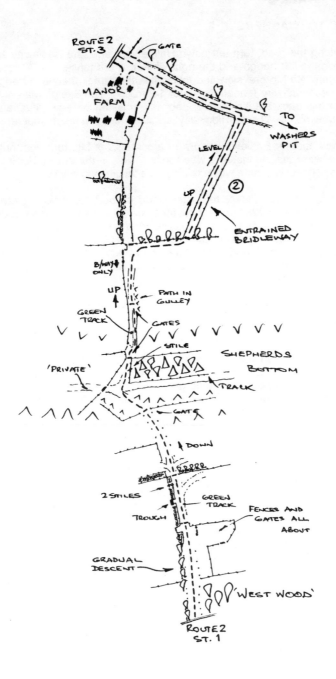

ROUTE 2 - STAGE 3

ASHMORE TO WASHERS PIT

Returning along the road, turn left down Halfpenny Lane, the Bridleway-signed track between the left hedge and the right white-painted fence.   Walk past the 'Bridleway Only. No Motors' sign and follow this long track, between hedges at first, until it becomes wire fenced for about 1/2 mile.   The Sketch Map reduces the length of this track but it's quite a long way, passing several gates, another Bridleway arrow and a 'Wessex Ridgeway' arrow, before you reach your turning.

When you find another Bridleway arrow on a post on the left, turn right onto the chalk track which runs alongside a wire fence.   This is the official Footpath so follow the track down to a gate which leads into a fascinating wood.

Known as Great Morris Close, this vast wood harbours coppiced hazel and ancient oaks together with beech, chestnut and pine trees.   The coppiced hazels were used mainly for fencing and pens for the vast flocks of sheep in this area.   Even at the time of the Domesday Book of 1086, there were 826 sheep in Ashmore - plus 50 goats and 27 pigs.   Now, the wood is filled with bird song, the argumentative cackling of crows and rooks, the screeches of pheasant and the overhead mewing of buzzards.

Before you go on - This being a working forest, the description of trees in the next Stages may not fit exactly what you encounter but the tracks themselves shouldn't change.

Follow the track through the deep wood to a junction of tracks and zig-zag right/left across.   There are signs of a lot of deer about as you descend slightly for the next 1/2 mile.   Soon, you emerge onto a wide and winding forest track where the Footpath continues straight on into a descending valley.   Join the forest track to the right of this Footpath and follow it around a long, almost 180º, right bend with mixed woodland on either side.   Enjoy the bird song as the track keeps bending this way and that for about 3/4 mile.

Eventually, your track meets another, even wider forest track coming from your left and signed as a Bridleway.   This is the main Stubhampton Bottom route from the River Tarrant valley.   Turn right onto this long, winding and slightly rising track which follows a wide valley with a couple of Bridleway arrows en route.

The sky is more open here and the walking is easy until, quite suddenly, you emerge, past a Forest Enterprise barrier, onto the Ashmore road.   This is Washers Pit so have a look at the notes in the Stage 4 text on the next page before you turn left up the road - but don't linger too long or you may feel a chill.

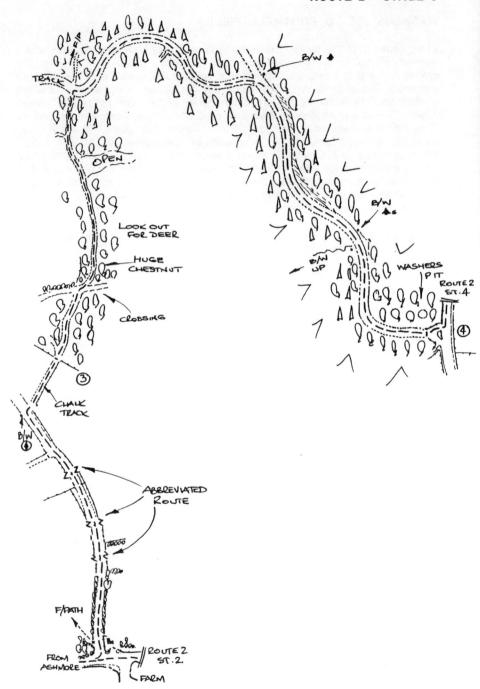

43

ROUTE 2 - STAGE 4

WASHERS PIT TO FONTMELL FIELDS

Strung out along this valley, there are several ancient, disused limepits which were once used for burning hair from hides of cattle and sheep.   Washers Pit stands in line with these and the weirdest tales of Ashmore are connected with this spot - O S Map Reference ST897168 (L V Grinsell's Barrow 3e).   Let me quote from E W Watson's 'History of the Parish of Ashmore 1651-1820' (dated 1890)   'There was another barrow, over which the road to Fontmel now runs, by Folly Hanging Gate, near Washers Pit.   In this lonely place, till within living memory, strange sounds were made by creatures in the air called Gappergennies, or however the name may be spelt.   When, perhaps 50 years ago, a metalled road was made to Fontmel instead of the old cart-track, this barrow, which lay close to the old road and on the line of the new one, was dug up, and the bones it contained buried in the churchyard....since then, the strange sounds have not been heard'.

Here, a woman was found hanging by her hair from a tree overhanging the now-vanished well.   She was cut down by a serving woman who was moved to visit the spot by three successive dreams.   Before you go - a woman in white is said to brush against travellers in the dark between Washers Pit and Spinneys Pond.

Now, continue up the road, past the gate into Shepherds Bottom and turn right into the Bridleway along the right edge of Fontmell Wood, noticing the old sunken track on your right which would go straight to Washers Pit if the new road hadn't cut through it.   Follow the Bridleway with a clearing on your left and Shepherds Bottom on your right.   The track bends as it begins a slight ascent with Scots pines, oaks and coppiced hazel and, approaching a mighty Scots pine on a right bend, you will see the ancient track in the coppice on your right.   At the next clearing, a steep track turns left up the hillside just before a deer fenced area with a blue, straight-on arrow painted on the corner beech tree.

Turn left up the hill track against the deer fence.   As a grass track goes off left, the fenced enclosure finishes as well and, a few yards further on, another track goes down to your right and you join the main track coming from your left.   Keep following the straight-on direction, past another blue arrow on a corner beech and an avenue of lofty Scots pines along the next left, wide track.   Still keep straight on, not so steep now, but still ascending with the skyline showing through the beech wood on your left and with thinner trees on the right slopes.

Another track turns off right, at the start of a bank and gully alongside your track on the right with a deciduous pine wood behind it.   Overgrown dyke, ancient track, deer defence bank or what?   Your guess is as good as mine.   Anyway, keep going, past another left turn and a right track beginning on the other side of the dyke.   There are now coppiced hazels on either side of the track and a field beyond the hazels on your left and, as the track widens, you go past two gates into the left field and a World War II shelter enclosed on your left amid some Scots pines and straggly beeches.   Now, after tracks to left and right, you arrive at 1.1/2 steel gates which bring you out onto the top Blandford to Shaftesbury road.   Go through the smaller gate and carefully cross the road to the Footpath-arrowed stile next to the gate in the opposite fence.

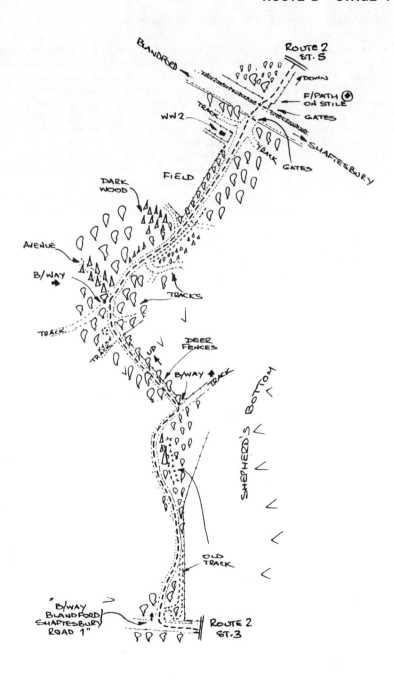

ROUTE 2 - STAGE 5

FONTMELL FIELDS TO SPREADEAGLE HILL

Over the wooden stile, there is a new wood on your left with older pine trees beyond them.   There is a field on your right with a fine view to Melbury Beacon. Follow the grass track away from the road and, as you descend, the path narrows and runs along the top of a ridge, bending around some older beeches.   Go down to the stile in the fence facing you.   The track which runs downhill on the other side would take you to Fontmell Magna.   Your route is the straight main track which comes from the left field gate and extends far to your right.   From this stile, you can see the Iron age hill fort of Hambledon Hill - more of which later. For now, turn right, with the field on your right and with the beech-clad slopes above Longcombe Bottom on your left.   Follow this track for a good 500 yards and you will arrive at a 1/2 gate into the right field and a stile next to a gate across your path.   Notices advise you that you are entering the 'Dorset Wildlife Trust Nature Reserve', management of which is '...Grant Aided by English Nature'.

Over this stile, another gate leads into the right, high field and you then drop down as the track turns sharply round to the left en route for Longcombe Bottom. Don't follow it!   Keep following the fenced field on your right by going up a steep bank, on a narrower path behind scrubby hawthorn bushes.   *Between the bushes, there are delightful views into the glorious, narrow-bottomed, steep-sided valley of Longcombe Bottom, beyond the valley to Hambledon Hill and across the valley to Fore Top and its cross-dykes.   These were probably more to stop cattle from wandering off the upper slopes than for defensive purposes.*

Anyway, enjoying the views on the last 1/2 mile of this lovely walk, keep on the narrow path until you reach a cattle trough.   From here, turn slightly down the slope towards a stile and gate in the facing wire fence.   The sign confirms that you are in the 'Fontmell Down Nature Reserve' but, still admiring the lovely view, cross the top field towards the left corner of the small, fenced pine wood.

Turning right around the wood's far side, walk up towards the grassy banks facing you, past the fenced turning between the two small woods.   Follow the next fence round to the 'Fontmell and Melbury Estates' notice and then head up to the far, top left corner of the field where you will find a 'National Trust Path' stile in the wire fence.   The road opposite follows the old Ridgeway which you crossed after the Airfield on your way into West Wood.

Over the stile, follow the left fence along the edge of the road for 1/4 mile back to the car park where you started.   *Before you go home, let me tell you about a link between Compton Abbas below you and Hambledon Hill.   During the Civil War, several of the local Royalist leaders were seized by Colonel Fleetwood during a secret meeting in Shaftesbury on August 2nd 1645.   Mr Bravel, the rector of St Mary's in Compton Abbas, was Commander of the Dorset Clubmen who met up on Hambledon Hill two days later to march on Shaftesbury to rescue them.   But Cromwell was already on his way to Shaftesbury with 1000 dragoons.   In the ensuing hour-long battle on Hambledon Hill, with between 2500 and 4000 Clubmen, 60 Clubmen were killed, 400 were taken prisoner (including 4 rectors and curates and 200 wounded) whilst the rest escaped to fight another day.   Of Cromwell's men, 13 were killed.*

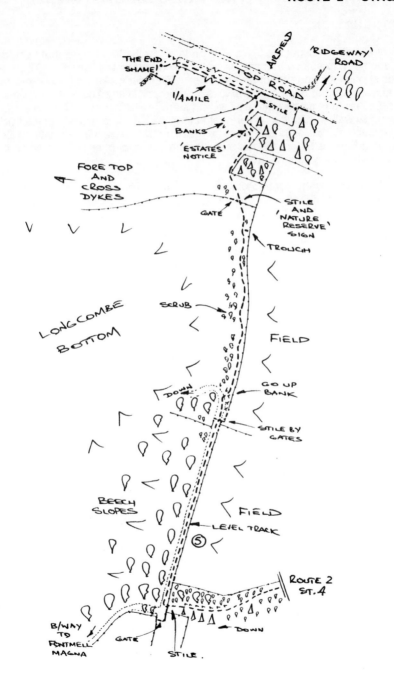

47

PART THREE - THE ABBOTSBURY AMBLE

INTRODUCTION

First of all, let me dispel the title's allusion to an 'amble'. It's just that I couldn't find another expression meaning 'a walk' which begins with an 'A'. This walk needs strong legs and proper hiking boots. For most walks in the countryside, I would never be happy in anything less than proper hiking boots although many people seem to manage quite well with trainers or wellingtons. There are steep hills on this walk and, in the winter or after long periods of rain, some of the tracks can be quite muddy. In particular, the descent from Abbotsbury Castle to East Bexington Farm is steep and notoriously slippery - except in summer when it is just steep and rough on the ankles.

Over the last thousand years, Abbotsbury has had only two owners. First there was the Abbey and then the Fox-Strangways family, the Earls of Ilchester. The Swannery has been maintained by the Strangways since the Dissolution of the Monasteries by Henry VIII. The 14thC St Nicholas' church stands close to the remnants of the Benedictine Abbey. The church was extensively rebuilt about the end of the 15thC whilst the chancel has a plastered barrel ceiling dated 1638. There is an effigy of a 12thC abbot in the porch and the Jacobean pulpit bears pistol-shot holes from a skirmish between the Roundheads and the Cavaliers.

St Catherine's Chapel stands, massive and conspicuous as a daytime guide to sailors and, when it was first built in 1370, it showed a beacon in times of storm .

Whether you come to Abbotsbury by car, bus or bicycle, the walks start opposite the 'Ilchester Arms' in Market Street (Reference SY576853 on O S Map No. 194), near the bus stop and not far from the car park which is next to 'The Swan' on the B3157 Eastbound. Several well-timed buses run to Abbotsbury. These include the First Southern National 210 from Bridport and Weymouth plus Rural Buses 63 from Wyke Regis and 1 from Weymouth and Dorchester in the summer.

THE ALTERNATIVES

Although there are several circular routes of varying lengths which you can choose as you circumnavigate Abbotsbury, I have detailed just two whilst pointing out a few shorter alternatives as you progress around the long Route 1. All Routes begin and end at the foot of Back Street, opposite the Ilchester Arms, because it is handy for bus stops and not too far from the car park.

ROUTE 1: Total distance 8.1/4 miles - This Route follows grassy paths and chalk tracks over high, breezy downs with great views of Chesil Beach, Portland, the coast in both directions and the sea. After you have seen the spectacular view from the top of Abbotsbury Plains, the trail heads inland to visit the prehistoric Grey Mare and Her Colts and the valley farm of Gorwell. It then returns to the ridge above Abbotsbury and follows the 'Inland Dorset Coast Path' for a while until you reach Abbotsbury Castle hill fort. Then, the Route turns down the National Trust's very steep Turks Hill to follow the unique natural structure of Chesil Beach. From there a Bridleway leads to a field path with super views of the Swannery. A steep ascent up the side of St Catherine's Hill leads to the 14thC Chapel before descending finally into the heart of Abbotsbury.

ROUTE 2: Total distance miles 4 miles - After Gorwell Farm and on attaining the heights of Wear Hill, this delightful walk leaves Route 2 and turns down the grassy hillside with lovely views. The easy track passes outcrops of sandstone and a small cliff of Abbotsbury iron ore. From there, the path descends further until it returns you into the village about 100 yards from the Ilchester Arms.

STAGE	MILES	TOTAL MILES
ROUTE 1:		
1 Abbotsbury to White Hill	1	1
2 White Hill to Gorwell Farm	1.25	2.25
3 Gorwell Farm to Wears Hill	1.25	3.50
4 Wears Hill to Turks Hill	.75	4.25
5 Turks Hill to Coastguard Lookout	1.50	5.75
6 Coastguard Lookout to St Catherine's Hill	1.50	7.25
7 St Catherine's Hill to Abbotsbury	1	**8.25**
ROUTE 2:		
Abbotsbury to Wears Hill as Route 1 - Stages 1 to 3 but only as far as the Abbotsbury return turn-off	3.25	3.25
3a Wears Hill to Abbotsbury	.75	**4**

ROUTE LAYOUT

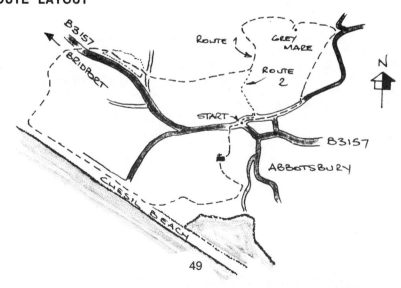

ROUTE 1 - STAGE 1

ABBOTSBURY TO WHITE HILL

Having made your way from the bus stop or the car park to the corner of Back Street, opposite the 'Ilchester Arms', walk up the lane past Strangways Hall and the Old School Tea Rooms.   Continue past the telephone box, the conveniences and the Old Chapel on the left side.   After some stone cottages, the first left turn is a Bridleway down which any short-cutters on Route 2 will be returning quite soon.   For now, continue up the lane, past 'Spring Cottage' and 'The Keep' on the left and a row of modern stone houses on the right.   With a gate leading to farm sheds on the left, Rosemary Lane on the right leads down to Abbotsbury car park and there is a banked and fenced field on the left side of the road.   Still going uphill, after houses on the right side and past Bishops Close, an overgrown hollow-way goes off to the left.   Just after that, you can accelerate to over 30 mph if you so wish.

The road bends left as a farm track bears off through gates to East Farm.   Keep going uphill for another 200 yards.   The road bends right towards a mixed wood but you turn off here, at a gate with a Bridleway sign for 'White Hill'.   A deep, steep, grassy track begins to climb up steeply.   After two cattle troughs, the track dog-legs a little to the left and keeps climbing upwards. Keep straight on up in the well-worn gullies.   *Take your time and you can get your breath back whilst admiring the wonderful views behind you which stretch along Chesil Beach to Portland and beyond along the Dorset coast.   Higher up, you can see all the way to Devon if it's a clear day.*

Slumped patches of hillside show the chalk which keeps this upland area relatively dry underfoot even in rain-sodden weather.   Nearing the top, a grass track comes from your left and crosses your path.   *The Bridleway signpost at this junction on your right points straight up the slope for 'White Hill' and right for 'Lime Kiln Car Park'.*   Keep straight on up the hillside, aiming for the top grassy gully.   Our route rejoins the road in a while.   *Clearly horses and carts (and hikers) can negotiate steeper slopes than cars because shallower slopes and a couple of bends had to be included when the tarmac road was built.*

The Hardy Monument, which is the huge stone tower that you can see from the top of the hill, commemorates the life of Thomas Masterman Hardy, Lord Nelson's flag captain at the Battle of Trafalgar who lived at Portesham, just two miles East of Abbotsbury.   This tower is visible for miles around and can be seen almost as soon as you enter Dorset from the Lyme Regis direction in the West or from the Yeovil direction in the North West.

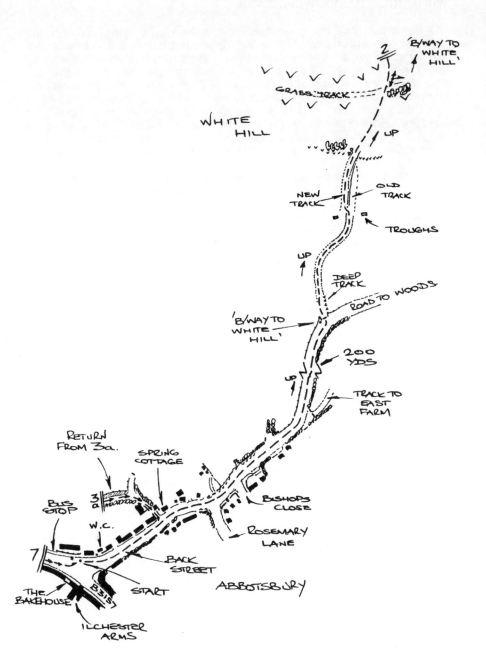

'B/WAY TO WHITE HILL'

GRASS TRACK

WHITE HILL

2

UP

NEW TRACK

OLD TRACK

TROUGHS

UP

DEEP TRACK

ROAD TO WOODS

'B/WAY TO WHITE HILL'

200 YDS

UP

TRACK TO EAST FARM

RETURN FROM 3a.

SPRING COTTAGE

BISHOPS CLOSE

BUS STOP

3a

W.C.

ROSEMARY LANE

7

BACK STREET

ABBOTSBURY

THE BAKEHOUSE

B3157

START

ILCHESTER ARMS

ROUTE 1 - STAGE 2

WHITE HILL TO GORWELL FARM

Still upwards, follow the green track into a deep gully between banks and lynchets.   As a faint grass track comes from your left, the trail becomes clearer and firmer with chalk and flints in the track.   Go through the Bridleway-arrowed gate into the top field.   Keep straight until you can see the left corner of the fenced field over the brow, next to a three-way Bridleway signpost.   You are now on the top of the ridge with the Inland Dorset Coast Path going off on your left to 'West Bexington 3.1/2'.   *If you like, you can follow this direction along the top ridge and you'll find that the path from Gorwell Farm meets you towards the end of Stage 3.*   The path you really want points, for now, to 'Hardy Monument 2' and the views across the patchwork of fields to Portland are outstanding.

The Bridleway follows the right fence and hedge on an ancient parish boundary bank.   This leads you down a sunken track to a half-gate exit onto the road that comes from Abbotsbury.   The signpost points back for 'West Bexington 3.1/2'.   Out on the minor road, follow it slightly uphill, past the right stile that turns off to 'Hardy Monument'.   After a passing place on the right, turn into the sharp hairpin lane turning on your left, following the field on your left and with a banked hedge on your right.   The lane soon zig-zags right/left after a cattle grid and gate which lead to 'Gorwell Farm Only - Camping and Caravan Club'.

For now, follow the chalky lane to its sudden right turn.   Keep straight on through the half-gate next to the farm gate marked with two Bridleway arrows and a sign for 'Kingston Russell Stone Circle'.   *There are so many circles, barrows, enclosures and earthworks around this small area - and the Valley of Stones between this spot and Little Bredy Farm - that it's a wonderful place to explore.*   In this high, level field with rough grass in front of the left banked hedge, follow the grass track past a 'Danger. Low-Flying Aircraft' notice until you begin to descend slightly and pass through an opening in the bottom corner hedge.   In about 15 yards, next to another 'Kingston Russell Stone Circle' sign, go over the footpath-arrowed stile in the left hedge and bear right to follow the facing hedge along the top slope of a valley which begins in this field.

Go through the first gate in the hedge to 'The Grey Mare and Her Colts'.   *This is a cromlech - a megalithic barrow built from pudding-stones. These are concretions of a gravel bed which cemented itself to the bed of chalk beneath.   Lumps of this stone fell into the valley and were collected for cromlechs and circles such as this one, Kingston Russell's and the Nine Stones at Winterborne Abbas.*

After viewing the stones, return through the gate and bear half-left, not along the top hedge but following the electricity poles down into the valley.   This line will carry you down to the bottom end of this long field.   Make sure that the solitary tree in a deep hole is up on your right as this will ensure that you follow the descending valley slope in the right direction.   Nearing the bottom, the valley becomes deeper and you reach a gate across your path.   Go through the gate between double fences onto a muddy (or rutted) track which approaches you from in front and turns to go up the right valley slope.   Go straight on down the track, with Park Coppice on the left slopes and a wire fence on your right, towards Gorwell Farmhouse ahead of you.

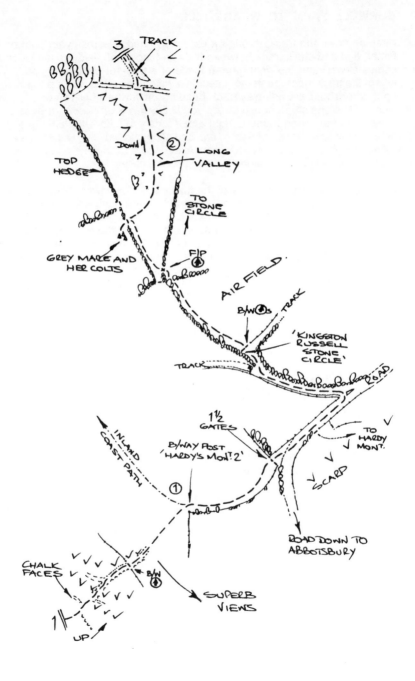

53

ROUTE 1 - STAGE 3

GORWELL FARM TO WEARS HILL

Keep on down the track, through a gate in the hedge across your path onto the firmer, flint and chalk track between the iron-fenced left field (as the wooded hill comes closer) and the right garden fence of a tree-surrounded house. At the end of the track, go through the gate into a wide open area with a paddock on the right corner and a Bridleway/track heading off to the right to Long Bredy (no sign). The fine stone house facing you is Gorwell Farmhouse. It boasts a vast assembly of assorted barns to right and left as you follow the lane up to the left between wooded slopes of beech, oak and coppiced hazel. The woods bear the names Park Coppice, Bow Coppice, Alley Moor, Bramble Coppice and Broad Coppice as you progress along the track up the valley.

A stream follows the right edge of the track/lane, now tarmac, and you will soon see the old grass-covered dam which formed a small pond with a central island on your right. After a wide verge on your right and a small brick shed, the lane bends left when the woods end but our route turns up the concrete track after the Bridleway-signed gate on your right. Follow the steep track between the wire fenced field and the coppice on your right. The fence soon ends opposite a right gate into a hedged field but the track keeps climbing through a pair of gates across your path. Through the second gate, follow the fence straight up and over the brow of the ridge. Drop down the other side to a collection of gates and a stile.

The left green track, before the fence, is the Inland Dorset Coast Path route again and comes directly from the Bridleway signpost on White Hill on Stage 1. Climb over the footpath-arrowed stile by the left gate onto the slopes of Wear Hill and turn right, sparing a few moments to enjoy the views along Chesil Beach, over St Catherine's Chapel and out to sea. *The path which turns left down the slope leads straight back to Abbotsbury and arrives in Blind Lane at Back Street near where you started. This is the shorter Route 2 down. If you want to go back now on* **ROUTE 2,** *turn to ROUTE 2 - STAGE 3a for details and the Map - but it's too nice to stop now.* The ridge walk to Abbotsbury Hill Fort is superb, the stroll along the seaside is gentle and salty and St Catherine's chapel is well worth a visit, so you'll be glad you stayed.

ROUTE 1: Turn right and follow the top fence, past the Bridleway signpost confirming the ways to 'Abbotsbury, Hardy Monument and Hill Fort'. After the first 1/4 mile of pleasant walking along the high greensward, you pass a cattle trough and another signpost that gives you another chance to take the quick return to 'Abbotsbury 3/4'. Then you arrive at a gate in the hedge and fence in the top corner. Go over the stile and keep straight on, enjoying the views with three barrows in the adjoining field.

There is a pond down below you for irrigation purposes. There are other wet areas on the slopes as well but these are caused by slumping (or gravity transport) - sudden, rapid soil movements caused by excessive water in the soil or clay which makes the earth behave as a liquid and to slide down the hill. The movements are easily recognisable by the wet hollows retained behind a higher bank on the downhill front.

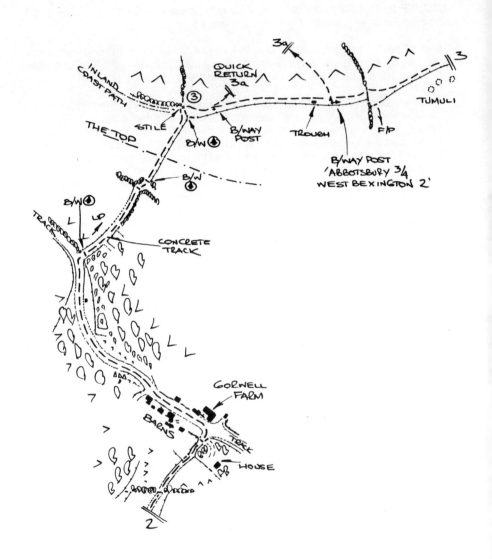

INLAND COAST PATH

3a

QUICK RETURN 3a

3

③

STILE

THE TOP

B/W ④

B/WAY POST

TROUGH

TUMULI

F/P

B/WAY POST 'ABBOTSBURY ¾ WEST BEXINGTON 2'

B/W ④

B/W ④

TRACK

L LD L

CONCRETE TRACK

GORWELL FARM

BARNS

TRACK

HOUSE

2

WEARS HILL TO ABBOTSBURY

ROUTE 2: This Stage is only for the short cut back to Abbotsbury.   Everybody else on the longer Route 1 will be on Stage 4 by now.

It won't take long from here back to the village so, as you'll be missing the long stroll along the ridge, why not spend a few moments enjoying the fabulous views from the stone seat to the right of your descending grass track?

Over on your left, you can see the Isle of Portland extending out into the sea. Long famous for its fine stone quarries which have provided much of the stone for buildings in London and other major cities, Portland also provided harbour facilities and a helicopter base for the Navy until it was closed down in 1995/96. It is sad that this lively adjunct to the Dorset coastal scene is no more and the skies are no longer filled with the buzz of oversized dragonflies.   Chesil Beach, the unique bank of shingle which stretches for some 16 miles from beyond West Bay to Portland, gradually increases in height from sea level at its Western origin to Portland where it is 50 ft high.   The pebble sizes are similarly graded from pea-size at Bridport to large cobbles at the Portland end and local fishermen claim that they would be able to tell exactly where they are along the beach if they were ever shipwrecked in the dark.

Now, back to your descent.   Turn down the sunken green track, starting at the tumulus, and follow it between banks, hollows, hummocks and outcrops of greensand to a junction of green tracks next to the farm gate in the first hedge. A signpost points back up to 'Hill Fort 1.1/4' whilst the gate carries a Macmillan Way arrow.   Through the gate, follow the raised track down to another Bridleway-arrowed gate in the top corner of a wire-fenced field.   Through this gate, follow the edge of the descending low ridge straight ahead, with more stone outcrops over on your left and with a valley dropping down to your right.   Go down past a signpost which points left to 'Lime Kiln Car Park' and past the banked corner of a recent planting of trees on your left.   Keep to the main track now, down past a rough path which heads into the right gorse-clad valley, following the left bank to a gate which leads onto a narrow path in a wide gully.

Just after the gate, you will notice that the soil and rock in the path is dark red. This is an exposure of Abbotsbury iron ore and, after a couple of trees on your left, you will find a deep red rock face where geologists from miles around hope to find fossils amongst the thin beds of hematite in the oolitic, sandy deposits.   As this iron is only a thin coating on the original sand grains, there is too much silica to make the iron profitable to extract.

Follow the path down, steep but soon firmer underfoot as it widens between fenced fields.   After two opposing gates and a right corner stile there is a fine view over the village below you.   Follow the flint track round to the left.   Continue down past 'Copplestone', the big thatched house on the next right bend, and past a track going up left to a paddock.   Now, with a ditch and hedge on your left, pass a thatched, stone shed and emerge out of 'Blind Lane to White Hill' next to 'Spring Cottage'.   You're now back onto the Route 1 - Stage 1 map for the last few yards to the start - not that you'll need to follow it very closely.

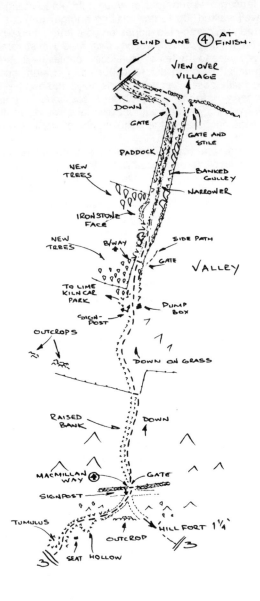

BLIND LANE ④ AT FINISH.

VIEW OVER VILLAGE

DOWN

GATE

GATE AND STILE

PADDOCK

NEW TREES

BANKED GULLEY

NARROWER

IRONSTONE FACE

NEW TREES

B/WAY

SIDE PATH

GATE

VALLEY

TO LIME KILN CAR PARK

PUMP BOX

SIGN-POST

OUTCROPS

DOWN ON GRASS

RAISED BANK

DOWN

MACMILLAN WAY ④

GATE

SIGNPOST

TUMULUS

OUTCROP

HILL FORT 1¼'

3

SEAT HOLLOW

3

57

ROUTE 1 - STAGE 4

WEARS HILL TO TURKS HILL

When the fenced field runs out on your right, keep straight on along the clear, wide and well-walked top route, passing another tumulus and a water tank on your right and with gorse-clad slopes on your left. *You will soon see the B3157 coming up the hill on your left - a fine coast road with several viewpoints along the way.* As you pass to the left of the electric cables post ahead, a Bridleway turns down to your left towards the road but keep straight on, past a left tumulus, another electricity post, a roofless stone shed and another left tumulus. *There are superb views into the valley of the River Bride on your right and across to Litton Cheney.* A large farm with its own lake lies down the right slopes as the path follows the right side of the ridge, cutting off your view of the sea for a while.

The ridge is much narrower now, with scrub prevalent on both sides, and you descend into a levelled grass area with a tarmac lane crossing the ridge ahead of you. Go over the footpath-arrowed stile next to the small gate and cross the lane to the sandy pull-in for cars opposite. Go up the sandy path in the left end of this lay-by, through gorse bushes, to find an Armada beacon next to the wire fence on the top. *This beacon is part of a chain of beacons which were lit in the 1988 national celebrations of the Defeat of the Spanish Armada in 1588. If you've been on 'The Blackmore Vale Path', you'll have seen the one on top of Okeford Hill.*

Zig-zag through the gorse to the footpath-arrowed stile in the corner and climb over onto the slopes of Abbotsbury Castle. You will find yourself on the seaward side, walking in the uppermost defensive ditch. Negotiate the dyke which crosses you path and immediately turn up the steep path on your right to reach the O S plinth set at 620 ft. From the plinth, follow the clear green path along the open, scrubby top of the ridge, immediately passing another right tumulus. *From here, there are excellent views ahead to West Bay and Bridport.* Past the remains of an ancient dry-stone wall and zig-zagging down and up another dyke, the path becomes gentle, downward, wide and grassy as the ridge runs out completely. Aim for the stile which you can see ahead of you in the corner, at the junction of the right dry-stone wall and the left road fence. The stile carries a Footpath arrow whilst the adjacent sign indicates that it is now only 1.1/2 miles ahead to West Bexington. *One side says it's 4.1/2 miles back to the Hardy Monument but the other side says it's 1/2 mile.*

Very carefully cross the B3157 and climb over the facing stile which stands at another dry-stone wall/wire fence junction. A National Trust sign informs you that you are now on the slopes of 'Turks Hill'. Follow the stone wall for 250 yards down the field to the corner where a signpost points left down to 'Chesil Beach 1'. *This is where you will need your best gripping boots if you're here during or just after a wet period because the clay and chalk are particularly prone to releasing ground water onto these slopes whilst the steep hillside path is tightly contained between the stone wall and the dense gorse.* So, gird up you loins and down you go!

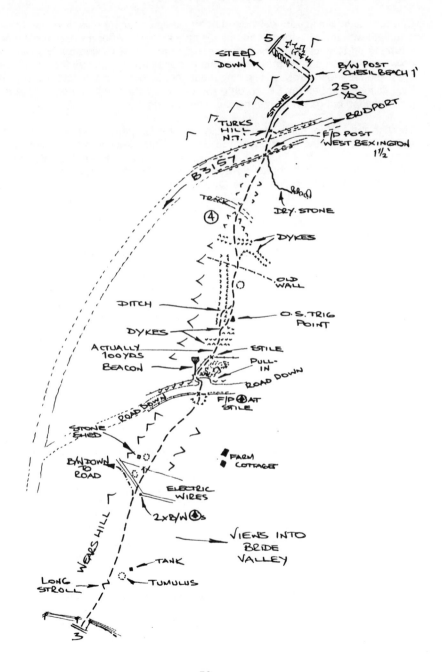

ROUTE 1 - STAGE 5

TURKS HILL TO COASTGUARD LOOKOUT

Carefully maintaining your balance - I hope - keep on for 1/4 mile down the gorse-clad path with the wire fence and bushes on your left. After a while, you'll reach a turning off to your right which is signposted for 'West Bexington' but keep on down, skirting around an intruding clump of hawthorns which causes you to lose the fence for a few yards. Rejoining the fence, go over the stile into a 200 yards long descending field and keep on down into the bottom left corner. There is a pine-shielded bungalow in the enclosure on your right.

Through the hedge, climb over the stile with the footpath arrow and aim for the right gable end of the farmhouse (165ºSSE). This direction will lead you to the farm gate, with another footpath arrow, in the bottom corner of this field, near a cattle trough. A ditch comes down the field next to the hedge and runs under the track on the other side of the gate. Join the track and follow it through another gate and around the outbuildings and barns of East Bexington Farm. As the firm track bends right past the barns, another signpost next to the hedge up on your left points back to 'Hill Fort' and on to 'Chesil Beach'. Cross the main farm track which leads to the farmhouse on your right and go into a downhill track with a Bridleway arrow on the corner post and a fenced paddock on the right.

Go through the gate at the bottom and bend right/left to follow the track down with a ditch and hedge on your right. As the hedge gives way to another fence, the track bends back left/right and leads you down to a short stretch of fenced track, over a main drainage ditch and onto the old tarmac lane which serves the farmsteads between Abbotsbury and West Bexington. The 'Coast Path' stone confirms that it is 1.1/2 miles back up to the Hill Fort and another 1.1/2 miles to West Bexington on your right.

The sea is very close at hand now but a brief diversion onto the shingle will convince you that it's too difficult to walk very far on it. So stay on the tarmac lane with the banked ditch on your left for 3/4 mile, passing several 'No Parking' passing-places on your right. There are many run-off ditches from the steep fields on your left joining the main ditch and running under the lane to beach outfalls. Alongside the second field ditch, a gravel drive turns up to Lawrence's Cottage (previously the East Bexington Dairy House).

Follow the lane and, after a beach access barrier, you meet a tamarisk hedge. *This is a salt water and wind-resistant, deciduous hedge with feathery branches and masses of pink flowers in the summer (Sorry, I mean 'abundant racemes of small flowers' - Royal Horticultural Society Encyclopaedia). There are plenty of these tamarisk bushes along this lane and all the way into Abbotsbury and St Catherine's Hill. They are quite a feature of the Strangways Estate.*

On the left side of the lane, the Coastguard Lookout stands next to the row of Castle Hill Cottages, their gardens and their garages. The ditch which had accompanied the tamarisk hedge has now crossed to the field side and soon disappears completely, only to reappear after the road T-junction. Pass the drive to the 'Old Castle Laundry' and cottage with a fine thatched barn.

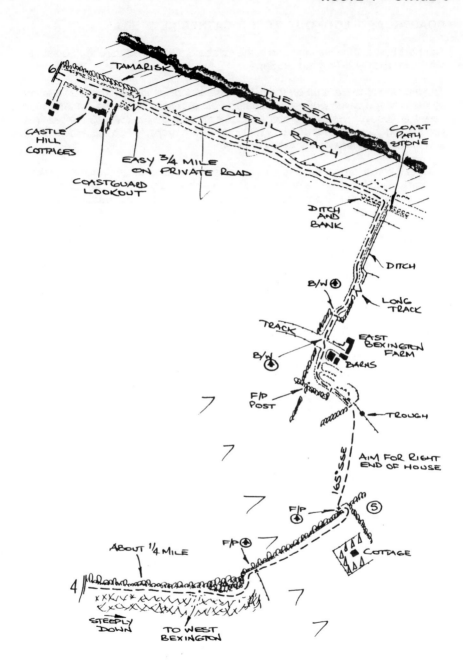

THE SEA

TAMARISK

CHESIL BEACH

6

CASTLE HILL COTTAGES

COASTGUARD LOOKOUT

EASY ¾ MILE ON PRIVATE ROAD

COAST PATH STONE

DITCH AND BANK

DITCH

B/W

LONG TRACK

TRACK

EAST BEXINGTON FARM

B/W

BARNS

F/P POST

TROUGH

AIM FOR RIGHT END OF HOUSE

165° SSE

F/P

⑤

F/P

COTTAGE

ABOUT ¼ MILE

4

STEEPLY DOWN

TO WEST BEXINGTON

ROUTE 1 - STAGE 6

COASTGUARD LOOKOUT TO ST CATHERINE'S HILL

The next field is 1/4 mile long and is the last before the direct road to Abbotsbury via the famous Sub-Tropical Gardens.

The broken stone walls up on the hillside are all that remain of an earlier attempt by the Strangways to build a castellated house in addition to the manor house near the Abbey. Sadly, the propensity for the soil to slide towards the sea (as you saw on your descent of Turks Hill) caused the property to be abandoned. It was almost completely demolished in 1934.

Now, call at the car park's cafe for a quick snack and at the convenient services for a wash and brush up before your return to Abbotsbury. From the car park, go over the footbridge to the shingle-covered lane which runs parallel with the beach. Turn left and follow the tamarisk hedge. *If you walk up the wooden ramp, you may be able to struggle along the top of the Chesil Beach for a few yards before coming back down to this track. You can get a better idea of the long sweep of the shingle from up there.*

Follow the track alongside the tamarisk hedge until, just before a path bears off into the 'Fleet Nature Reserve', you get a brief view of St Catherine's Chapel across the lynchets in the field over the hedge on your left. *As you get nearer to the Chapel, the hill becomes too steep to see it and, when you emerge onto the hilltop, its great bulk comes as something of a surprise.*

At the Coast Path signpost, follow the direction for 'Abbotsbury 1' and 'Swannery 1.1/4' along the track which bends left to a gate onto a fence- enclosed track. In a few yards, a farm gate leads into the low field between the Bridleway and the reed beds. Follow the track along the hedge until you reach a large ditch/stream which runs under the turning to the right gate. Keep straight on for another 100 yards, passing between the left tamarisk and the right bushes which keep you away from the stream. A signpost on your right indicates the Bridleway straight on into Abbotsbury and over the stile to the Swannery.

Climb over the stile and follow the right fence up towards a World War II pill-box in the adjacent field. Follow the edge of this rising field up to a gateway in the top corner with lovely views of the Fleet and the Swannery ahead of you. Through the gate, follow the path along the slopes of St Catherine's Hill. You pass a post with an acorn emblem, another WWII pill-box, another acorn and a footpath arrow post. Then, you reach a stone which turns you left onto the steep, winding path up the red-soil slopes and lynchets. Take plenty of stops on the way up.

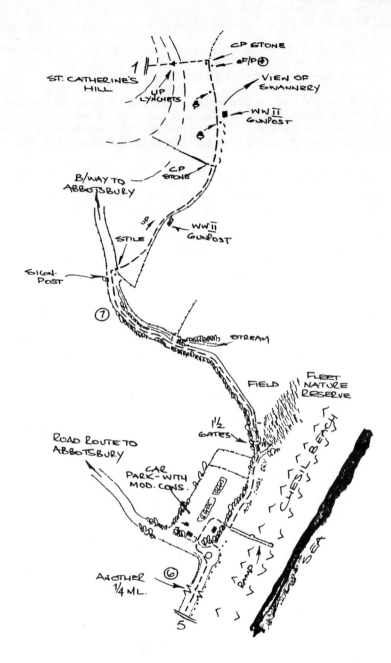

CP STONE
● F/P ⊕
1
ST. CATHERINE'S HILL
UP LYNCHETS
VIEW OF SWANNERY
WW II GUNPOST
CP STONE
B/WAY TO ABBOTSBURY
STILE
WW II GUNPOST
SIGN-POST
⑦
STREAM
FIELD
FLEET NATURE RESERVE
1½ GATES
CHESIL BEACH
ROAD ROUTE TO ABBOTSBURY
CAR PARK-WITH MOD. CONS.
SEA
RAMP
ANOTHER ¼ ML.
⑥
5

ST CATHERINE'S HILL TO ABBOTSBURY

Keep straight up the steep grassy banks and pass within about 20 yards of the wood on your right. A direction of 320ºNW will lead you the right way - otherwise, just follow the clearest path straight on up the hill.

Nearing the top, you cross a narrow dyke and a green track which comes from your left. Out of breath, you will be quite unprepared for the sudden appearance of St Catherine's Chapel and, as you approach the stile towards its left end, the sandstone structure with its 4 ft thick walls begins to loom massively ahead.

It was built either during the time of Abbot Henry de Thorpe who died in 1376 or Abbot William Cerne who ruled the Abbey between 1376 and 1401. At the Dissolution of the Monasteries in 1536-39, it was spared from demolition and stone-robbing because of its use to sailors as a conspicuous landmark. It was needed as much by Henry's own navy as it was by trading vessels and local fishermen. The chapel is dedicated to St Catherine, a high-born, scholarly lady of Alexandria who, for her faith, was tortured on a wheel and then beheaded in 290 AD during the reign of Emperor Maximinus. Her awful death is commemorated on 15th November each year.

Leave the chapel by the corner kissing gate and join the grass and red-soiled track to descend towards the dry-stone wall. With fine views over Abbotsbury village and Abbey ahead of you, follow the track past the kissing gates in the stone wall and round its bottom end where it bends left and continues to descend, passing two cattle troughs and a walled enclosure of stone barns and a long shed on your left.

Go through the kissing gate and join the track which arrives between the barn walls and a high banked field from your left. Follow the track straight on with a stone wall on your right and a banked field on your left. Where a gate and stile lead up into the left field, the bush-covered path on your right leads to the back of the 'Ilchester Arms'. Keep straight on, past a gated house drive and between stone walls, to emerge between a handy shop and the Pottery onto the pavement of West Street. There is a small, iron-fenced garden with a couple of benches opposite your emergence so, if you have any sandwiches left, you could sit there and finish them off before your final end-of-day collapse.

Really, you could pop down to The Bakehouse for a sausage roll or savoury pastry and come back here to sit quietly awhile before going for your bus or your other transport. Relax and remember some of the wonderful sights you have seen today. You could plan to come back and explore further another time.

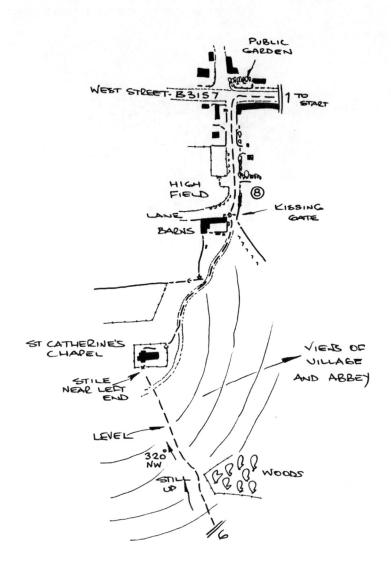

PUBLIC GARDEN

WEST STREET · B3157

1 TO START

HIGH FIELD

⑧

KISSING GATE

LANE

BARNS

ST CATHERINE'S CHAPEL

VIEW OF VILLAGE AND ABBEY

STILE NEAR LEFT END

LEVEL

320° NW

STILE UP

WOODS

//6

CIRCULAR DORSET RAMBLES

Top: St Catherine's Chapel, Abbotsbury. Page 64

Bottom: Smedmore House, Kimmeridge. Page 80

PART FOUR - THE ENCOMBE ENCOUNTER

INTRODUCTION

How could any book purport to introduce anybody to the delights of Dorset without including at least one walk in the Isle of Purbeck? I firmly believe the panorama from Swyre Head is the most wonderful sea, cliff, down and farmland view anywhere in this beautiful county. Paragliders launch themselves from the slopes of Smedmore Hill to fly with the crows and kestrels who regularly patrol these hills in search of food. They must all enjoy the superlative views along the Purbeck coast and savour the tranquillity as they glide over a pair of Purbeck stately homes - both of which you will see from similar high vantage points.

Kingston and Kimmeridge churches are both well worth visiting. Kimmeridge village benefits from an excellent and very popular tea shop/restaurant which is frequently packed in the summer and much patronised by climbers, hikers, geologists, sub-aqua divers and wind-surfers at all times of the year.

The longer Route 1 brings you close to the first on-shore oil field to be developed on this coast - but don't worry. All that is visible is a nodding donkey and a couple of small collection tanks inside a wire-fenced enclosure. This isn't the only industrial venture to be based at Kimmeridge. The shale has been known to contain oil for centuries. Actually, with the cliffs sometimes spontaneously igniting, it would be difficult not to notice. Earlier exploitation caused the bankruptcy of one Sir William Clavell whose tower is prominent on the cliff edge. Actually, his attempts at alum production and glass-making didn't help his finances or his desire to give employment to the people of Purbeck either.

For your complete enjoyment, I have introduced alternative Routes which will enable you to plan long or short walks or to change your mind on the way round.

THE ALTERNATIVES

Starting and finishing outside the 'Scott Arms' on the top of Kingston Hill (Reference SY956796 on O S Map No. 195), all three of the Routes share the first few Stages but diverge either at Swyre Head or Kimmeridge for the long or short variations as listed. Wilts and Dorset buses 143 and 144 from Poole and Swanage call frequently at the 'Scott Arms' so access for non-drivers is good.

ROUTE 1: Total distance 8.3/4 miles - This is the 'Total' Route which starts along the high lane from Kingston to the gates of the Encombe Estate, follows tracks and high grassland to the most magnificent view from Swyre Head's barrow and then swings West to follow the top of Smedmore Hill all the way to Kimmeridge. This charming little village, with its church, Post Office and Tea Rooms leads to the cross-fields path to Kimmeridge Bay whence your Route turns up to the cliff top 'Dorset Coast Path' route for two miles to Houns Tout. To be perfectly honest, Houns Tout rises 400ft from the cliff top at the end of the Encombe Valley and it isn't gradual, if you know what I mean. It's rather hard (Well, it makes the heart pound a bit and the legs begin to give out) - so you've been warned. The final leg of Route 1 is along a wide, gentle greensward above Encombe House and valley and through mixed woods back to Kingston.

ROUTE 2: Total distance 5.1/4 miles - After following Route 1 to Swyre Head, this Route turns down the steep slope of Smedmore Hill and crosses farmland of Swalland Farm to meet the cliff top route of the 'Coast Path' and Route 1 again for the climb up Houns Tout and back to Kingston. It therefore shares the steep climb up Houns Tout which I would only recommend for fitter walkers.

ROUTE 3: Total distance 6.3/4 miles - After leaving Route 1 at Kimmeridge, this alternative follows the valley lane between Smedmore Hill and the sea to visit Smedmore House and Swalland Farm on the way back. To avoid the Houns Tout climb, Route 3 brings you back up the side of Smedmore Hill to Swyre Head. Although it isn't as steep or as high as Houns Tout, this requires some degree of fitness as well. Apart from this climb - 350ft but with only the last 150ft being very, very steep - this is a comparatively easy Route which offers magnificent views on the way.

STAGE	MILES	TOTAL MILES
ROUTE 1:		
1 Kingston to Encombe Gate	1	1
2 Encombe Gate to Swyre Head	1	2
3 Swyre Head to Kimmeridge Hill	1.25	3.25
4 Kimmeridge Hill to Cliff Top Car Park	1	4.25
5 Cliff Top Car Park to Clavell's Hard	1	5.25
6 Clavell's Hard to Rope Head Lake	.75	6
7 Rope Head Lake to Houns Tout	1	7
8 Houns Tout to Encombe Wood	1	8
1 Encombe Wood to Kingston	.75	**8.75**
ROUTE 2:		
To Swyre Head on Route 1 - Stages 1 and 2	2	2
2a Swyre Head to Swalland Field	.25	2.25
6 Swalland Field to Rope Head Lake	.50	2.75
To Kingston on Route 1 - Stages 7,8 and 1	2.50	**5.25**

STAGE	MILES	TOTAL MILES

ROUTE 3:

To Kimmeridge Hill on Route 1 - Stages 1 ,2 and 3	3.25	3.25
4 Kimmeridge Hill to Smedmore Gates	.25	3.50
4a Smedmore Gates to Smedmore House	.75	4.25
2a Smedmore House to Swyre Head	.75	5
To Kingston by walking back on Route 1 - Stages 2 and 1	1.75	**6.75**

ROUTE LAYOUT:

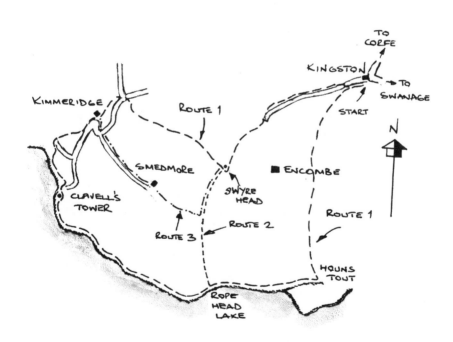

69

ROUTE 1 - STAGE 1

KINGSTON TO ENCOMBE GATE

Listed in the Domesday Book as Chingestone (the king's village), Kingston was leased to Shaftesbury Abbey and 200 years later it was known as Kyngeston Abbatisse. Kingston stands on the edge of the folded chalk Purbeck bed, looking down on the ruins of Corfe Castle and the lovely stone village which grew up around the castle, parts of which date back to pre-William the Conqueror.

Start outside the 'Scott Arms', facing the opposite side of West Street.   Turn right up the hill to the Post Office which stands on the elevated stone pavement opposite South Street.   St James' Church stands high in the churchyard on the far left corner at a height of nearly 450 ft.   *Its size appears over-generous for the population of Kingston when it was finished in 1880 after seven years' work for stonemasons and the local quarry.   It is one of the last churches designed by G E Street and it is built of the local Purbeck and Portland stone with a vaulted chancel and a lofty central tower.   The fittings are also by Street and the wrought ironwork is very fine.   It appears that the quarry's customers went elsewhere during the building of the church, never to return, and quarrying in Kingston came to an abrupt end when the church was finished.*

Carry on up West Street, past the last cottages and a forest track on your right, into the forested lane where your speed is now unrestricted.   Kingston House drive turns sharply down to your left whilst the left fork is the return route from the Coast Path and Houns Tout for both Routes 1 and 2.   The text covering this return is in Stage 8 but it'll be quite clear when you're ready for it.   Now, keeping straight on, (signed for Encombe House), you pass 'The Plantation' car park with mixed woods on either side.   After a pair of 'Private' tracks into the woods, you leave the stone wall-enclosed woods and the road continues, slightly up and down, across a vast sloping field for about 1/2 mile with fine views right to Corfe Castle and the twin chalk ridges, one each side of the castle.

After a couple of passing places and a few lonely hawthorns, you will see a 40ft obelisk.   *This was erected in 1835 ....'in honour of Sir William Scott, created Baron Stowell'.   The first stone was laid by Lady F I Bankes, younger daughter of John Scott, the 1st Earl of Eldon who bought Encombe House in 1807.   Now you know where the 'Scott Arms' connection fits into the Encombe Estate.*

There are tempting views ahead to the barrow on Swyre Head, just past the left end of the woods which run along the top of Encombe Valley.   The beech wood over on your left is growing on the nearer slopes of the same valley.   After the slight left bend in the road, the road descends between a low left field edged with a row of beech bushes and trees and a right fenced and stone walled field.   Keep on down to the end of this field and, level with the gate into the next right field there is a car parking area on your left.   A stone plaque in the corner gives some detail about the Coast Path.   The road continues towards 'Orchard Hill Farm' but you have to turn left, down through the stone pillared gateposts, signed for 'Encombe House and Lower Encombe'.   Through the gateway, keep straight on - not down the long 'Private. No Footpath' drive but across to the sheep pens, the farm gate and the smaller gate with the 'Dogs on Lead' sign .   This gate leads onto an uphill, stony farm track in a wide, grassy sheep-grazing field.

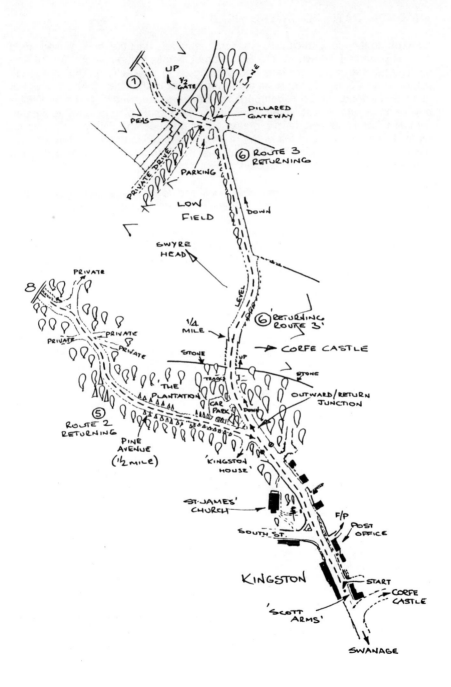

① UP ½ GATE

LANE

PENS

PILLARED GATEWAY

⑥ ROUTE 3 RETURNING

PRIVATE DRIVE

PARKING

DOWN

LOW FIELD

SWYRE HEAD

LEVEL

⑥ 'RETURNING ROUTE 3'

→ CORFE CASTLE

⑧ PRIVATE

PRIVATE

PRIVATE

PRIVATE

¼ MILE

STONE

STONE

UP

THE PLANTATION

TRACK

OUTWARD/RETURN JUNCTION

⑤ ROUTE 2 RETURNING

CAR PARK

DOWN

PINE AVENUE (½ MILE)

'KINGSTON HOUSE'

ST·JAMES' CHURCH

F/P

POST OFFICE

SOUTH ST.

KINGSTON

START

CORFE CASTLE

'SCOTT ARMS'

SWANAGE

ROUTE 1 - STAGE 2

ENCOMBE GATE TO SWYRE HEAD

Keep on up the stony track with grass up the middle until the stone-walled wood over on your right, known as 'The Belt', comes across to meet you. On the way up, you pass a couple of grass tracks going up to your left and the wire fence comes across to meet your track in the top corner of the field. At a junction of gates and wooden fences, go through the Bridleway-arrowed half-gate and sit for a while on the stone seat on the other side. Another track turns down to a gated field and then continues down a grassy gully into Encombe Valley. Stay up on the high greensward and follow the dry-stone wall along the valley top with the mixed 'Polar Wood' behind it. This wood is filled with bluebells in late spring and they are at just the right eye level to look like a blue mist.

Now, with Encombe House, its stable block and its walled gardens appearing at the foot of the slopes on your left, perhaps a little detail wouldn't go amiss. The property was sold to George Pitt of Stratfieldsaye (The 1st Duke of Wellington's home from 1817) in 1734 but he died the same year and the house passed to his son, John Pitt - an amateur architect. Using ideas from the Palladian style and from the works of Vanbrugh and Hawksmoor, John redesigned the house and it was rebuilt by 1770, retaining some of the original property. John's son, William Moreton Pitt sold the house to John Scott, later 1st Earl of Eldon, in 1807 and, since 1870, under John, 3rd Earl of Eldon, extensive internal alterations were made. The stables are early 19thC and were built by the 2nd Earl of Eldon.

Now, enjoying your stroll along the top of the valley, the greensward soon includes a track but just keep going, very slightly uphill now. After a stone step into the woods, the track bears left round the head of the valley towards the back of 'Swyre Wood'. As the track disappears, keep swinging round to the left and you will find a marker stone between you and Swyre Head bowl barrow. *The Royal Commission on Historical Monuments advises us that this barrow stands more than 600 ft above sea level, that it is 83 ft diameter and 8 ft high .* The stone says that it is 2 miles back to Kingston and 1.3/4 miles to Kimmeridge. Walk over to the stile in the far fence and be prepared for a breath-taking coastline view. I've seen it several times but it never fails to send a tingle down my spine. *A stone seat just past the barrow gives you a fine opportunity to savour the view and, when you have imbibed fully, you have to decide whether to continue to Kimmeridge or take the shorter Route 2 straight down to the Coast Path and return via Houns Tout.*

From the stile, I'll assume that you are going straight on - *so Route 2 walkers scan down to your instructions in italics.* Follow the fence and then the stone wall across the level field. Go through the 1/2 gate with the Bridleway arrow into the next field, keep following the wall down and go through another half-gate next to a farm gate which leads onto a fence-enclosed, rutted grass track.

ROUTE 2: *Turn left and go over the stile onto the Footpath-signed slopes of Smedmore Hill. Carefully descend the gorse-clad path into a wide, bumpy field of coarse grass and sheep until your route is edged by wire-fenced fields.*

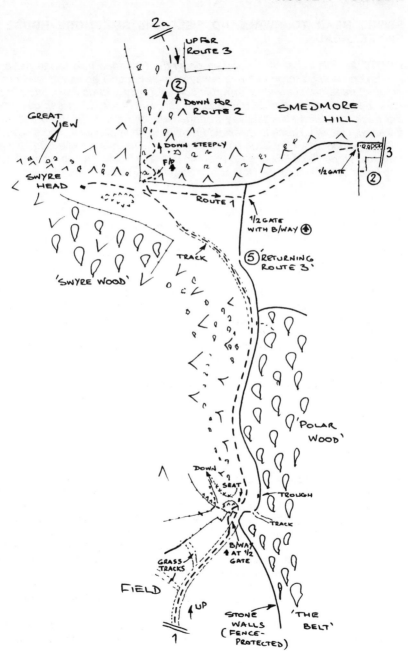

2a

UP FOR
ROUTE 3

(2)

DOWN FOR
ROUTE 2

SMEDMORE
HILL

GREAT
VIEW

DOWN STEEPLY
F/P

R.POST

3

½ GATE

(2)

SWYRE
HEAD

ROUTE 1

½ GATE
WITH B/WAY

(5) RETURNING
ROUTE 3

TRACK

'SWYRE WOOD'

'POLAR
WOOD'

DOWN

SEAT

TROUGH

TRACK

B/WAY
AT ½
GATE

GRASS
TRACKS

FIELD

UP

1

STONE
WALLS
(FENCE-
PROTECTED)

'THE
BELT'

73

ROUTES 2 AND 3 - STAGE 2a

SWYRE HEAD TO SWALLAND FIELD and SMEDMORE HOUSE TO SWYRE HEAD

ROUTE 2: (Still in italics)   Keep on down the fenced-in field to the narrowing bottom end and go through the gateway or over the stile on its left.   Cross the group of tractor tracks with a farm track on your right and go down into a rutted, grassy, fence-enclosed track past another stile and gateway.   Keep going down the track to a third stile/gateway arrangement and into a T-junction of tractor tracks with the main track to Swalland Farm down on your right.   There is another stile to the right of a very large gate facing you.   This has a stone sign for 'Coast Path and Rope Head Lake'.   Go over the stile and follow the right banked hedge and fence down the field.   Now turn to Stage 6 to continue - still in italics.

ROUTE 3: Keep straight on, with the walls of the kitchen garden on your left and the white-railed gateway into 'Smedmore House Camping and Caravan Site' down on your right.   A 'Private' drive turns away to your left after the garden walls and you now continue up the lane with a hedge, then a small wood, on your left and with a ditch and mixed trees on your right.

Slightly uphill, with overgrown fences to right and left, the right verge widens at the top of the slope and there is a gate into the right field.   Descending now, the lane bears left as you reach gated fields either side, just before 'Chaldecotts' - the house on your left.   Keep going, uphill slightly again, over a ditch which runs from and into overgrown, scrubby patches and climb up towards Swalland Farm with a hedge on your left and a fence on your right.

Walk carefully through the barns and cow-sheds of Swalland Farm, now on concrete, and past the farmhouse and its low-walled garden on your right.   The concrete now gives way to a rising, stony, chalky track between a left wire fence and a right hedge with a track turning into the right field.   Keep on up the steepening track until a stile turns off to your right, with a sign for 'Coast Path and Rope Head Lake'.

Walk into the junction of tractor tracks and turn left, past a stile and an open gateway, into a fence-enclosed, rutted track.   At the end, go past another stile/gateway into a tractor-rutted area with another farm track going to your left. Keep straight on up, past a third stile/gateway into a widening, marshy and bumpy field of rough grass.   As the left fence ends, keep going up the very steep side of Smedmore Hill .   Follow the thin, bending path through the gorse bushes to the top fence where you will find a footpath-arrowed post and a stile in the top corner.   Go over the stile and you're back on Swyre Head.

Have another sit on the stone bench you found earlier.   You've earned it.

When you've rested, just go back to Kingston the way you came this morning - using ROUTE 1 - STAGES 2 and 1 in that order if you can't remember the way.

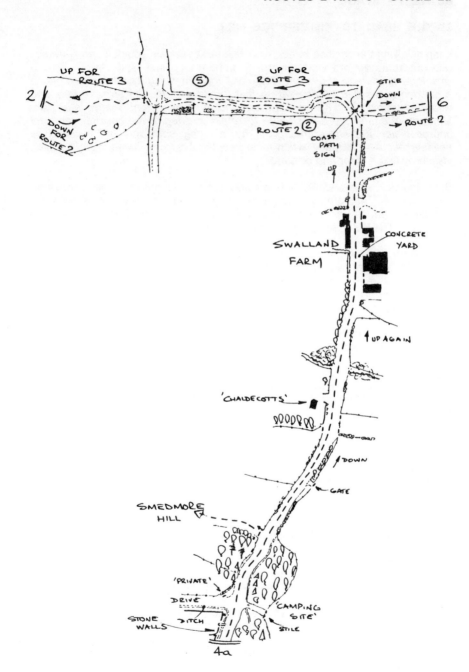

SWYRE HEAD TO KIMMERIDGE HILL

Keep following the enclosed track, now with hawthorns on your left and generally with the same superb view towards Tyneham Cap and Gad Cliff. *These limestone cliffs stand above the village of Tyneham which was evacuated by the Army during the 2nd World War so that they could use the area for tank and weapons training. They're still there and the small, stone village is in ruins although attempts are being made to retain and repair the buildings and the church which are still standing. It's a lovely spot and much visited by holidaymakers. Actually, when most people have gone home, it's also much visited by foxes, deer and buzzards.*

But I digress. After a while, there are some steps over the stone wall which lead onto a signed footpath to Smedmore. Where the path emerges onto the Smedmore road below, there used to be a sign which pointed unequivocally 'To The Top of The Hill'. Sadly, it has now disappeared.

Keep going and, after a bend to the left, a gate in a stone wall crosses your path, after which another gate opens onto the slopes on your left. You are now out of the enclosed track and in a stony field which drops down to the right and also straight ahead to another gate in a facing stone wall. Go through this gate into a steeply rising field and follow the wall up to the top. After a level stretch, with views ahead and slightly right to Steeple Church in the valley and Creech Arch on the top of the ridge beyond, the field begins to descend. From here on, it's all downhill into Kimmeridge village.

Go through the gate onto another fence and wall-enclosed, rutted, stony track which descends ever steeper around a right and left bend. On the way, you pass a scrub and gorse-packed area on your left but keep clear. Somewhere in there is the top edge of a quarry which opens out onto the road down into Kimmeridge. Follow the track around the left banked and right fenced bend to the bottom and go through the final gate.

At a junction of tracks, go straight down into a tarmac lane and turn left, between banked bushes on your left and the ditch and hedge on your right. Follow the lane down to a T-junction with a 'Farmhouse B & B' sign on the right corner. The left turn goes to the quarry and Kimmeridge by road but cross straight over to the stile which is signposted 'Kimmeridge 1/4'. The half-gate just up the hill leads onto the footpath to Tyneham Cap and village.

Go over the Kimmeridge stile and head down the bush and gorse-bordered grassy gully which brings you out onto the steep slopes of another sheep field. Aim for the gate in the iron fence, just to the left end of the church below.

St Nicholas' church is very small, very old and built of rubble stone with ashlar edges to doors and windows. The nave is 12thC and the 13thC South porch is original. The bellcote and buttresses were added to the West end in the 15thC whilst the church was extensively rebuilt in 1872.

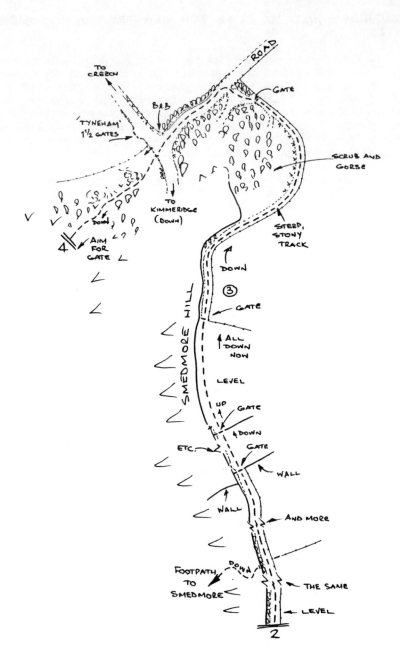

ROUTE 1 - STAGE 4

KIMMERIDGE HILL TO CLIFF TOP CAR PARK or SMEDMORE GATES

Go through the iron kissing gate after the ditch footbridge and walk down the 'slippery when wet' stone flagged path of St Nicholas' churchyard with the fence and stone wall of 'The Old Parsonage' on your left. *This fine stone house was built in 1837 in the 17thC Jacobean style.* Down the steps, a wide track goes right into Kimmeridge Farm. *The front entrance of Kimmeridge Farm house carries the shield-of-arms of Mansel - predecessors of the owners of Smedmore House.* There is a seat tucked into the stone wall on your left where you can think about which way you're going back from here.

ROUTE 3: If you want to go back to Kingston without using the Coast Path or the steep climb up Houns Tout, keep going left along the rising road, past The Old Parsonage gates, and keep straight on when the road does a hairpin left. Follow the hedged and fenced lane to the white gates which are signed 'Private Road. Smedmore and Swalland' and turn to Route 3 - Stage 4a which is just for you.

ROUTE 1: If you're going all the way on the longer Route 1, follow the road down into Kimmeridge with the walled playing field on your right and the Seven Taps Restaurant, Tea Rooms and Post Office on your left. *(I can recommend the cream teas - whatever the time).* The next left gate leads to the Village Hall, from where a footpath runs across fields to join the Smedmore track on Route 3 if you change your mind. If not, keep on down with stone, thatched cottages on your right and houses behind hedges on your left. When there are no more cottages on your right, go over the footpath-signed stile into a field which runs down by the garden fence of the last cottage. Follow the garden fence down to a footbridge across a stream with a stile at either end. Over the shady bridge, another stile leads into trees on your right but turn left here and follow the winding ditch, past a wood and a streamside row of willows, to a pair of footpath-arrowed stiles close to a low, ruined stone barn in the brambles and bushes on your right.

Over the stiles, keep following the ditch, with a fenced field beyond it, to another stile and a farm gate. This time, there is a small, fenced enclosure of dense bushes with a less ruinous barn perched on the far edge. Over the double footpath-arrowed stile, go past the barn and follow the tree-bedecked, winding ditch past one final left gate. Zig-zag right/left up, past a sunken ditch which comes from across the field on your right, to go through a footpath-arrowed farm gate and join the lane to the Oil Extraction enclosure. On the hawthorn-edged lane, turn left at the signpost 'Beach and Coast Path' and go through a gate which crosses the lane just before handy conveniences on your right. A stile in the left fence only leads up to the Toll Road.

Up the lane, follow the right bushes round into the car park and stroll around the seaward end, past or stopping at any loitering Ice Cream vans. At the far end of the car park, go through a narrow, 50 yards long gap between the bushes shielding the house up on your left and the edge (bushed or clear) of the cliffs on your right. Emerging into the divers' and sail-boarders' car park, there is a path down to the quay and the beach immediately on your right but, for the Coast Path, you have to go straight on through the parking area.

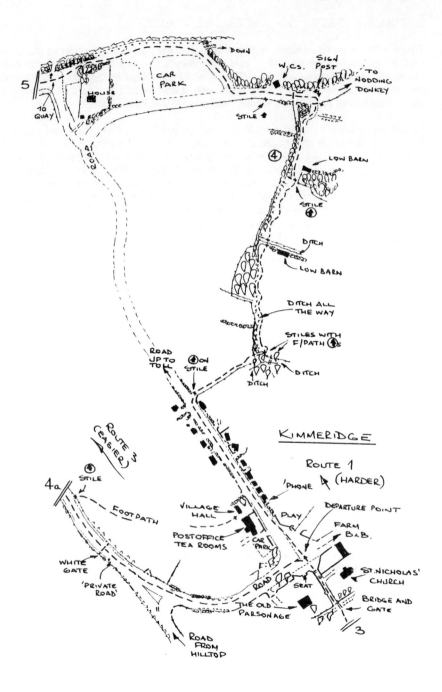

5

TO QUAY

ROAD A.1

DOWN

W.Cs.

SIGN POST

TO NODDING DONKEY

HOUSE

CAR PARK

STILE ↑

④

LOW BARN

STILE ↑

DITCH

LOW BARN

DITCH ALL THE WAY

STILES WITH F/PATH ④s

ROAD UP TO TOLL

④ ON STILE

DITCH

DITCH

DITCH

KIMMERIDGE

ROUTE 3 (EASIER)

ROUTE 1 ↑ (HARDER)

④ STILE

4a

FOOTPATH

'PHONE

DEPARTURE POINT

VILLAGE HALL

PLAY

FARM B.&B.

POST OFFICE TEA ROOMS

CAR PARK

WHITE GATE

'PRIVATE ROAD'

ROAD

SEAT

ST. NICHOLAS' CHURCH

BRIDGE AND GATE

THE OLD PARSONAGE

3

ROAD FROM HILLTOP

ROUTE 3 - STAGE 4a

SMEDMORE GATES TO SMEDMORE HOUSE

There are fine views of Kimmeridge village and the sea from this part of the lane and, as you're on your way back, you may fancy a cream tea. I can recommend the Seven Taps Restaurant, Tea Rooms and Post Office in the village so, if you go over the stile which you have just passed and head back across the fields, you will come out at the Village Hall, next door to the Post Office.

However, if I keep sending people to Kimmeridge Post Office, there will come a time when I won't be able to get a cream tea there myself because there won't be any room. So forget it and keep on going, with the lane descending a little around a slight left hand bend and with fenced fields on either side. After gates on your right and a gateway on your left, a stream comes out of the narrow wood on your left and runs into the left ditch. Another gate opens into each of the left and right fields before the lane passes a couple of hawthorns in the wider RIGHT verge. As a ditch crosses under the road, the right, wide grass track leads to 'Barn Dairy' farmhouse and barns.

Now, keep on going with a ditch, fence and hedge on your left and a verge, fence and hedge on your right. When another ditch runs under the lane from the edge of some trees on your left into a tree-lined ditch on your right, you go between two large Scots pines into the drive proper of Smedmore House. The tarmac drive ascends between grass verges and wire fences with stiles into private fields, passing a bulky, round yew tree on the way. Reaching the top of the slope, Smedmore House looks superb, grand but not over-grand. *It was built in the 17thC by Sir William Clavell of stone with a stone slate roof. Entirely remodelled in the early 18thC, the 'new and sophisticated South West elevation' was added. This includes the lovely rounded bow window elevations which are facing you. A new range of reception and entrance rooms were built across the North West end in 1761 and a kitchen wing was added. On rare occasions, Smedmore House opens its gardens to the public under the National Gardens scheme. If you get the chance to visit, do so. It'll be a splendid afternoon and you'll love the friendly and intimate gardens.*

Now, follow the lane around to the right, away from the house with some fine pine trees in the lawn near you. A track turns off right, alongside a mixed deciduous and pine wood, down to a gated field entrance. Keep straight on with a ditch and the stone garden wall of Smedmore House on your left. The low wall grants lovely views of the tree and shrub-planted garden on the South side of the house.

Now turn to Routes 2 and 3 - Stage 2a to continue along the lane for your Route 3 return to Swyre Head

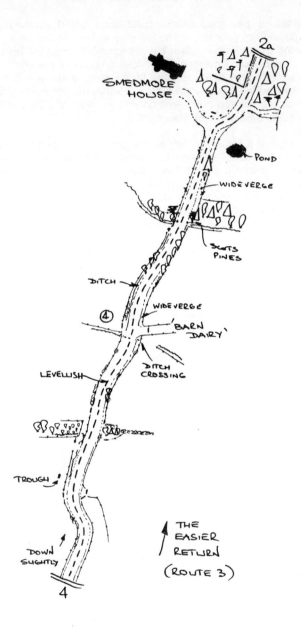

SMEDMORE HOUSE

2a

POND

WIDE VERGE

SCOTS PINES

DITCH

④

WIDE VERGE

'BARN DAIRY'

DITCH CROSSING

LEVELLISH

TROUGH

DOWN SLIGHTLY

4

THE EASIER RETURN (ROUTE 3)

81

CLIFF TOP CAR PARK TO CLAVELL'S HARD

Leaving the car park past another toilet block, turn down the tarmac track which comes down from your left.   The signpost in front of the bank of trees points the way for the Coast Path.   Over the stream, walk down the hill and past the right turn into the bottom Emergency Services and divers' car park.   After the World War II concrete tank defences, turn up the steep steps which are cut into the left hillside by another Coast Path sign.   At first, the steps wend their way through dense bushes but you soon emerge into the light at a fenced left field and with the cliff edge quite close on your right.

This is a bit of a struggle after all the gentle, level or downhill, strolling you've enjoyed so far, so take it slowly.   After a few more scattered steps and uphill climbing on grass, the field fence turns left and you're almost within gasping distance of Clavell's Tower.   *Have a good look around the tower and enjoy the views across Kimmeridge Bay, busy with windsurfers, rock pool explorers, divers and geologists.   It's not just the view, of course.   It'll give you an excuse to get your breath back - **but keep away from the cliff edge**.*

This is the first warning about the cliff edge but when you realise that the wire fence replaces earlier fences which have had to be moved back to accommodate the ever-retreating Coast Path, you'll have some idea of how unstable are these cliffs of Kimmeridge clay. The circular tower, a folly, was built by the Rev John Richards, who assumed the name of Clavell on inheriting Smedmore in 1817 and died in 1833.   It is built of brick and rubble-stone and rendered.

Now, continue past the Coast Path sign-stone which tells you that this cliff top path leads to 'Chapmans Pool 3.3/4'.   *You will be turning off the Coast Path back to Kingston before it reaches Chapmans Pool - but only just before - so you're in for a most enjoyable coastal walk with beautiful sea views and interesting rock strata in the cliffs from time to time, with the mingled calls of gulls on the seaward side and skylarks over the fields.*

I'll keep written instructions to a bare minimum along this section of the walk because of the proximity of the high cliff edge but suffice it to say that the path follows the contours of the land, crosses emerging streams as they plummet over the edge, and sometimes hugs the fence where more recent landslips have brought the cliff edge too close to the path.   To follow the text, stop to read it occasionally.   Let caution be your watchword - but enjoy it!

When you arrive at a short section of narrow-gauge rail track hanging over the cliff edge, you have arrived at Clavell's Hard.   *This little piece of track is a remnant of a 19thC construction used for transporting bituminous shale which Clavell mined here to boats waiting below near the cliff face.*

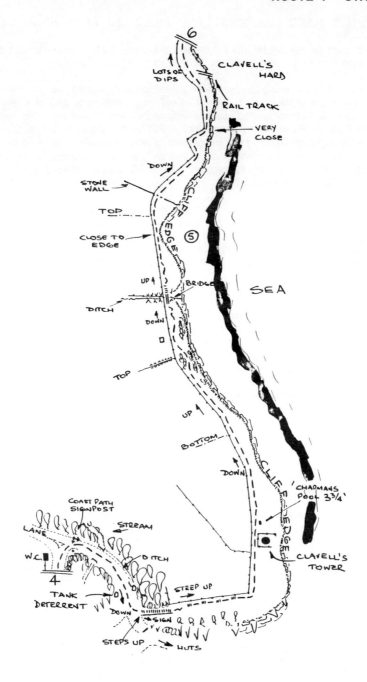

ROUTE 1 - STAGE 6

CLAVELL'S HARD (and SWALLAND FIELD) TO ROPE HEAD LAKE

This first part *(in italics)* is only for those on **Route 2** who came straight down from Swyre Head on Route 2 - Stage 2a without going to Kimmeridge:

ROUTE 2: *Keep following the banked right hedge and fence down to a dip in the field and then continue up and over a rise until you pass scrub and an overgrown hedge near the bottom end to reach a stile in the cliff top fence.   Go over the stile and turn left to join Route 1 walkers - at POINT * in the last paragraph on this page.   I've already warned the others not to go too near the edge of the cliffs because they're not very stable - as shown by the ever retreating fence and the brief explanation given two paragraphs down on this page.   Near the cliff edges, don't walk along whilst reading!*

ROUTE 1: After the rail track, a short descent brings you to one of the ditches as it runs out from the field and plunges over the cliff edge.   This one has a footbridge with a handrail on the cliff side.   After the bridge, go up and over a hump and you'll see another footbridge down the dip ahead of you.   There is a deep, grassy slump here where you can stop for a while for a read - it seems quite stable at the moment.

If you look at the bed of the stream between the bridge and the cliff top, you'll see that it is running on top of the smooth limestone layer.   This shows why the cliffs are so unstable.   They consist of smooth, flat layers of this limestone between layers of bituminous shale and Kimmeridge clay.   The first contains oil and the second is excessively slippery when wet.   Water percolates through the shale and soaks into the clay but stops when it gets to the stone bed, lubricating the joint between the stone and the overlying clay/shale.   Its own weight is enough to propel it downwards and outwards whenever the adhesion gives way.

'In the 17thC, Sir William Clavell proposed to extract alum from the layers of bituminous shale and also to use it, as the Romans had done before, as fuel for boiling sea water to extract salt.   These enterprises, and plans to manufacture glass, using the shale for fuel, came to nothing.   In the 19thC oil was, for a time, extracted from the shale, and an Act of 1847 gave powers to construct railways....inclined planes, causeways etc': D Maxwell's Unknown Dorset 1927.

Now, carry on up and over a long hill with some sections quite close to the edge. On the way down you will meet with the Route 2 walkers who come down the field to the stile next to the direction stone which says 'Kimmeridge Bay 1.1/2 and Chapmans Pool 2.1/4'.   *This is called Rope Head Lake - in recognition of Clavell's plans for a rope-making industry.   However, the flax needed for making the rope did not grow here very well and another bright idea bit the dust.   There is a small pond in the field between here and Swyre Head.*

POINT *:   Right then, **ROUTES 1 AND 2** should be all together again.   Go down the hill to a rough section where a ditch runs under the footbridge and out to the cliff edge.   On the other side, the cliff top is a bit wider at first and, after a bend in the fence where the edge comes closer, the climb becomes steeper.

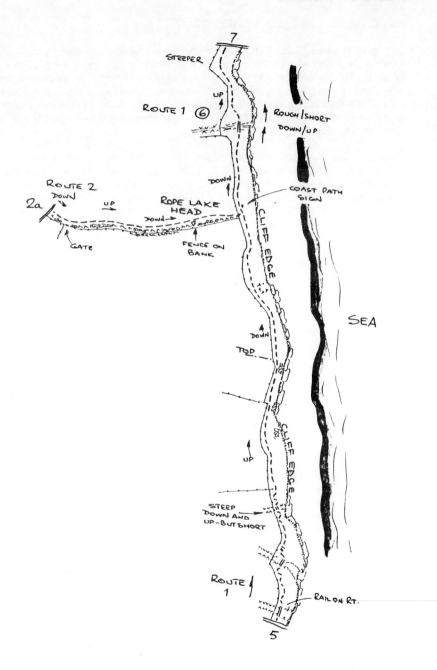

7

STEEPER

UP

ROUTE 1 ⑥

ROUGH/SHORT
DOWN/UP

ROUTE 2
DOWN

2a

UP

DOWN

ROPE LAKE
HEAD

COAST PATH
SIGN

DOWN

CLIFF EDGE

GATE

FENCE ON
BANK

SEA

DOWN

TOP

CLIFF EDGE

UP

STEEP
DOWN AND
UP - BUT SHORT

ROUTE
1

RAIL ON RT.

5

85

ROUTE 1 - STAGE 7

ROPE HEAD LAKE TO HOUNS TOUT

Descending again, cross a dry run-off and then a remnant of stone wall. *If you look forward and slightly left, you will see Eldon's Seat on the top of the hill.* When the land levels out, there are two more gullies about 50 yards apart in rough grass and, when the fence bends left, you drop down into a wide, rough grassy area with a field facing you on the opposite slope. Wend your way through the grass, veering towards the cliff, and climb up between the field and the cliff on a wide, grassy slope.

The slope becomes steeper until, at the top, Eldon's Seat is just along the edge of the fenced field away on your left. *The seat is made from a single block of limestone 8 ft by 4 ft with a second slab set up on edge to form a backrest, all on a stone podium. It was laid by Lady E Repton, elder daughter of the 1st Earl of Eldon, on 15th October 1835. Beside it is a memorial stone to Lord Chancellor Eldon's dog, Pincher, dated 1840.*

Now, enjoy the next 1/4 mile descent because you're coming to the promised struggle up Houns Tout. Descending steeply at first on grass, then up out of a small dip, the path levels out before descending once more, ever more steeply, until you reach the bottom where Encombe Valley arrives at the sea from its uppermost reaches near Encombe House. The valley is wooded and a stream which runs from the lakes is entrained within a stone culvert underneath the old drive. Then, it runs out over the surface of the natural stone bed to drop down a waterfall onto the beach. *It is strange to see a pair of stone gate pillars with rusted iron fencing right on the edge of a drop over the cliff edge but this was once another entrance to Encombe Valley from a carriage drive which came round the cliffs from Chapmans Pool around this headland. When you look at the massive slumping and landslips beyond the waterfall, you will get some idea of just how much land has disappeared over the years.*

May I suggest that you sit and ponder for a few minutes - getting ready for the steep and tiring climb up Houns Tout.

Ready? Turn away from the cliff and keep following the Coast Path along the coast, through the trees and bushes and up a zig-zagging line until you come out onto open ground again with another field on your left. *The trees on your left continue all the way along the side of the valley to where you entered the estate through the Encombe Gates earlier today.*

Use the slumped ground as steps and keep climbing the bush-covered slopes. There is a little respite as the path drops briefly into a rough grassy area with much slumping of the whole cliff between you and the sea.

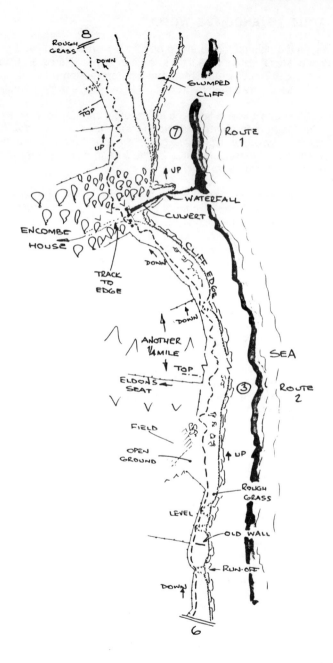

ROUTE 1 - STAGE 8

HOUNS TOUT TO ENCOMBE WOOD

Now you begin the ultimate climb of the day.   The area is wide and grassy with some slumped 'steps' but there is little else I can say.   However, take it slowly and look at the outcrop of weathered limestone on the top edge of Houns Tout overlooking the sea.   As it gets nearer, you'll know you're getting nearer the top.

Passing a section of old iron railing, you join another wire fence as you zig-zag up the hill.   *The Stage map shortens this bit just to make you feel that it's shorter than it really is.   However, when you get to the top, there is a wonderful, level and grassy stroll back to Kingston and, by the time that you reach the other end, you'll have fully recovered from this climb.*

At the top, there is a stone seat for which thanks are due to Mr Byrne.   *Resting here, you can see the Norman chapel on the cliff top at St Aldhelm's Head.*   When you get up again, you will find the Coast Path stone indicates '1.3/4 miles to Kingston', '3 miles back to Kimmeridge' and '2.1/4 miles to Swyre Head'.   Turn back to the stile in the corner between the fence and the dry-stone wall and climb over onto the wide greensward at the top of Encombe Valley.   *The easiest part to walk is about 20 yards from the wall as you follow the edge of the ridge back home and there are several stone blocks near the gorse-bushed slopes so you can make as many stops as you wish.*   Around the sweeping bend, go over another stile next to a farm gate in the wire fence and keep following the wall.

There are fine views of Encombe House, the stables, the walled garden and the lakes as you enjoy the gentle stroll.   Soon, a clear track follows the ridge and, after another stile and gate, it bends round to the right, following the wall to one last stile and gate which leads into Encombe Woods ('The Plantation').   The woodland track passes an opening into a right field and the drive of 'Hill View' house, becoming broken tarmac for a while on the way.   Keep following the track and......

ROUTE 1 - STAGE 1 (Part) - ENCOMBE WOODS TO KINGSTON

I know you'll forgive me just this once - but there isn't enough space next to the Stage 1 map for the text to cover the last few steps back to Kingston so read on here whilst referring to the other map - Thank you.

......passing a bank on the left side, you join a wider 'Private Property' track which comes in from your left whilst a Footpath sign points back to Houns Tout. Follow the dirt track round to the right, past more 'Private' tracks to left and right and keep following the main one, again signed for 'Kingston' as it turns into a cypress-lined avenue for about 1/2 mile.   This brings you to two short paths on the left - the first into a field and the second into 'The Plantation' car park . Immediately after these, you rejoin the lane which led you out of Kingston earlier today.   So go down and catch your bus, or get your car, or have a quick top-up at the 'Scott Arms'.   *It's been a grand Day, hasn't it?   If you didn't go all the way to Kimmeridge, you really ought to come back another day and use the Stage maps to devise your own, shorter circular walks.*

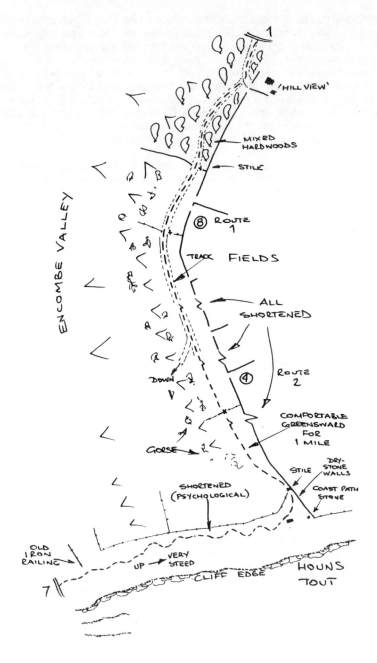

ENCOMBE VALLEY

1

'HILL VIEW'

MIXED HARDWOODS

STILE

⑧ ROUTE 1

TRACK FIELDS

ALL SHORTENED

ROUTE 2

④

DOWN

COMFORTABLE GREENSWARD FOR 1 MILE

GORSE

STILE

DRY-STONE WALLS

COAST PATH STONE

SHORTENED (PSYCHOLOGICAL)

OLD IRON RAILING

UP → VERY STEED

CLIFF EDGE

HOUNS TOUT

7

89

PART FIVE - THE MELBURY MEANDER

INTRODUCTION

A truthful title this time, these two walks - which when done together add up to the third walk - really do meander along some of the most peaceful valleys and low chalk hills, through villages remote from the busy main roads and in the grounds of a pair of fine country houses.   All three Routes begin in Evershot.   Route 1 starts immediately with a walk up the long drive to Melbury Sampford, the manor house of the Strangways family, the Earls of Ilchester who - you will recall from the Abbotsbury Amble - are the lords of Abbotsbury as well.   Evershot gets its name from *Eafor's holt*, the wood of the wild boar, and Leland called it 'a right humble and poor market town', the market then being held on Saturdays.   The manor was bought in 1761 by Stephen, Earl of Ilchester.

The second, and utterly charming, stately house is on Route 2 at Chantemarle. Built in the 15thC and added to in the early 17thC, it was used as a Police training college until quite recently.

THE ALTERNATIVES

Our starting point in Evershot is outside Moorfield House near the entrance to the Park (Reference ST576047 on O S Map No.194).   First National Bus 212 from Dorchester and Yeovil stops at School Corner in Evershot and Rural Bus No. 211 calls from Maiden Newton on Thursdays.

ROUTE 1: Total distance 5.3/4 miles - This Route begins with a 2 mile stroll through the Park of Melbury Sampford, the seat of the Earls of Ilchester, with its ancient oaks and a deer herd which dates back at least two hundred years. *Thomas Hardy's mother was born in Melbury Osmond and had been a servant in the house of a relative of the Earl of Ilchester in Maiden Newton.   She married Hardy's father at Melbury Osmond's church.   He had walked the 20 miles from Puddletown with his best man the day before the wedding.*   From the church, the Route crosses farmland and meadows to ancient woods and the hamlet of Melbury Bubb.   The historic church of St Mary the Virgin demands a visit before the journey continues into the bird-filled woods of Bubb Down and then returns along delightful estate tracks through meadows and mixed woods to Evershot. There are a few hills on this circuit - but not too strenuous if you take your time. The steepest section is Bubb Down Hill which is about 1:3 for about 150 feet.

ROUTE 2: Total distance 4.1/2 miles - Starting from the same point, this Route turns South and heads out of Evershot along fine downland farm trails on the Macmillan Way to the lovely house of Chantmarle and its charming grounds. Then, the Route takes you to the delightful village of Frome St Quintin and the pretty St Mary's church .   After a glimpse of the superb 18thC country house, you return through another farm to Evershot.   Although this is an undulating walk, the inclines are mostly gradual and any hills are relatively easy.

ROUTE 3: Total distance 10.1/4 miles - When you get back from the fine excursion of Route 1 and you can't wait until another day to finish the Melbury Meander, keep going and follow Route 2.   This is the 'complete' Route 3.

STAGE	MILES	TOTAL MILES

ROUTE 1:

1 Evershot to Melbury Park	.75	.75
2 Melbury Park to Melbury Osmond	1	1.75
3 Melbury Osmond to Church Farm	1.25	3
4 Church Farm to Bubb Down Plantation	1.50	4.50
5 Bubb Down Plantation to Evershot	1.25	**5.75**

ROUTE 2:

1 Evershot to Fortuneswood Farm	1.25	1.25
2 Fortuneswood Farm to Chantmarle	.75	2
3 Chantmarle to Frome St Quintin	1	3
4 Frome St Quintin to Burl Farm	.75	3.75
5 Burl Farm to Evershot	.75	**4.50**

ROUTE 3:

Route 1 - Stages 1 to 5 plus Route 2 - Stages 1 to 5	**10.25**

ROUTE LAYOUT

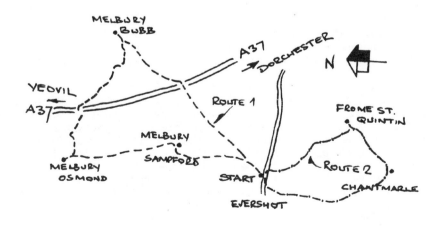

ROUTE 1 - STAGE 1

EVERSHOT TO MELBURY PARK

Arriving at the bottom of West Hill, or parking your car on the edge of the road which leads to the Ilchester Estate, set out along the 'Private' tarmac drive/Footpath passing the stone Swiss-style Cottage on your right.   You pass a pair of stone mullioned cottages on your left and, after a gate into the left paddock and a short path up the bank to the high right field, the grass-verged drive is edged by new framed trees and a high hedge.   *The first lane on your right, with a banked left corner and a right gate, is the Bridleway down which you will be returning from Route 1 - Stage 5 so make a note of it.   When you arrive back at this junction, you'll be able to find your way back to the start, won't you?*

Now, continue up the lane until, at a left muddy track, the high right bank gains a stone wall which accompanies you all the way to the entrance to Melbury Park. A tree-filled hedge follows the drive on your left to the stone-built Park Lodge with its ornamented gateposts and a cattle grid across the road.   A short track turns up to the right where a stile leads you safely over the stone boundary wall into the Park.   *You now have the prospect of a fine, free walk through the Park with its magnificent old trees, lovely Melbury Sampford house and its herd of deer.* Walk up the drive and over the brow of the hill.   Descending now, a gate in the right deer fence leads onto a grassy, pine-lined track whilst a turning bears off to the left, signed 'Lodge Farm Only' and 'Don't Disturb the Deer'.

Walk down to the kissing gate, signed 'Public Footpath', next to the cattle grid and enter the part of the Park where you may well encounter the deer.   *I once arrived here in early spring just as the deer were being called for feeding.   Most of them were together in the Park area ahead on the left but two enormous, off-white stags with the most incredible antlers suddenly burst from the woods on the right and charged off to get some feed.   They looked more like elk than deer - well, the deer that I was used to meeting in Dorset, anyway.*

Carry on down the track with excellent views of Melbury House over on your right. Pass a right track returning from the valley and a track on your left which leads up to Lodge Farm.   The surrounding trees are mostly very old oaks, chestnuts, beeches and pines and, as you reach the bottom of the slope, the ground on your right is somewhat marshy.   After some yews on the left, a 'No Right of Way' track turns left, vaguely towards the lake.   Keep straight on up the main drive.

Through the trees on your right, you can still see the original sandstone building of Melbury House which, according to Coker, used '3000 loads of free-stone fetched from Hamden quarry, nine miles away'.   The manor is in the Domesday Book as Meleberie, held by Roger Arundell.   Thomas Strangways and his wife Eleanor came from the Manchester area and their son Henry was the first of the family to come into possession of Melbury Sampford by a will dated 1504.   His son Giles, whilst extending this house, also added the Park and bought the Abbotsbury estates featured in 'The Abbotsbury Amble' from Henry VIII for £1096.10.   When you reach the best public viewpoint for the house, the most prominent section is that built by Sir Giles Strangways in the late 17thC whilst its best prospect is that facing East towards the little 'ancient but neat pile' of the 15thC church.

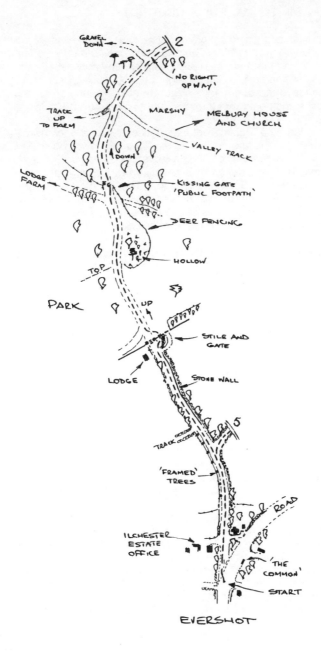

GRAVEL DOWN

2

'NO RIGHT OF WAY'

TRACK UP TO FARM

MARSHY

MELBURY HOUSE AND CHURCH

VALLEY TRACK

DOWN

LODGE FARM

KISSING GATE 'PUBLIC FOOTPATH'

DEER FENCING

HOLLOW

TOP

PARK

UP

STILE AND GATE

LODGE

STONE WALL

5

TRACK (cross)

'FRAMED' TREES

ROAD

ILCHESTER ESTATE OFFICE

'THE COMMON'

START

EVERSHOT

93

ROUTE 1 - STAGE 2

MELBURY PARK TO MELBURY OSMOND

Keep on up the drive, passing several turnings to yards and service buildings for the Manor House on your right. *There is open parkland on your left, the most likely area for seeing the deer, but keep going as they only usually approach the drive when it's feeding time.* Go through the high kissing gate next to another cattle grid and leave the deer park. You are now entering an area with wood-fenced paddocks and again with turnings right to more service buildings.

The drive turns left by a 'Public Footpath' notice. *A look back over the double gates which lead onto the lawned front of the house will give you some idea of the magnificence of this noble edifice. The elevation facing you is fine enough but, if you look beyond it, you will be able to make out the original dark sandstone tower of the first Melbury Sampford House. The old building dwarfs the 'new' section which faces you whilst, over on its left you will see the little 15thC stone church. The church register dates back to 1580 and the Strangways have been buried here since Dorothy Strangways was the first in 1592.*

Now, walk away from the house and keep straight on, past a turning to your right . In the open park, the drive has an avenue of old oak trees and newer trees in frames ready for when the old oaks are no more. Keep straight on for 1/2 mile to a gravel track bearing right. *This must have been the main drive at one time because the avenue of old oaks follows this direction, not ours, and it leads to the Drive End exit from the Park.* But keep straight on. There have been lovely views towards Melbury Osmond along our drive. At the end of the drive, there is another gate and another cattle grid. Go over the stile into a fenced area with a handy seat and an opening back into the lane on the other side. Follow the lane down alongside the high, hedged field on the left and past the turn into Townsend Dairy yard on your right.

The lane bends left to pass in front of Townsend Dairy House. Follow the lane past the thatched cottage facing you and another pretty cottage on your right. Walk round a left and a right bend with banked hedges either side and keep descending, past the turn into two cottages down on your left and then with a stream running alongside the left side of the road. *When you've visited the Church of St Osmund, you'll have to come back here because the unsigned track before the cottages on your right leads to Stage 3 and the path to Melbury Bubb.*

For now, keep on down to the ford which runs between Chapel Cottage on the left and Bridge Farm on the right and use the footbridge on the right to get past it. Begin to ascend with Riverside Cottages on your left and, after a grassy track on your right, Bridge Farm Cottage and a row of fine stone cottages also on your right. After a left turning and the stone-mullioned Old Post House on your right, you reach the stone-walled garden of the Old Rectory, also on the right, whilst a stone wall leads the road around the top left hand bend. St Osmund's now faces you. *It was rebuilt in 1745 by Susanna Strangways Horner in the Georgian style.. 'presenting no points of interest. The best part is the handsome monument in various marbles on the South wall of the chancel, describing the piety and munificence of Mrs Strangways Horner and her liberality to the poor' : Rev Hutchins, not me.* Return to Bridge Farm for Stage 3.

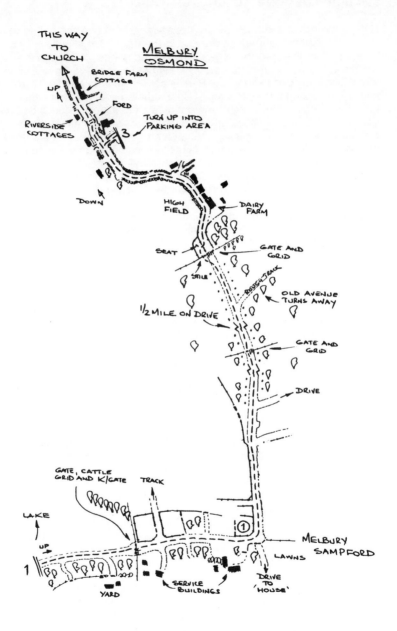

THIS WAY
TO
CHURCH

MELBURY
OSMOND

BRIDGE FARM
COTTAGE

UP

FORD

TURN UP INTO
PARKING AREA

RIVERSIDE
COTTAGES

3

DOWN

HIGH
FIELD

DAIRY
FARM

SEAT

GATE AND
GRID

STILE

OLD AVENUE
TURNS AWAY

1/2 MILE ON DRIVE

GATE AND
GRID

DRIVE

GATE, CATTLE
GRID AND K/GATE

TRACK

LAKE

UP

1

MELBURY
SAMPFORD

LAWNS

YARD

SERVICE
BUILDINGS

DRIVE
TO
'HOUSE'

95

ROUTE 1 - STAGE 3

MELBURY OSMOND TO CHURCH FARM

Having turned up the track by the cottages, go through the half-gate at the far end of the communal parking area.   In the field, bear slightly left past a horse trough and walk across to the gap in the facing hedge.   Through the hedge, you will, be in the old avenue of Melbury Park not far from the Drive End exit.   The stile which you need to leave the Park is not visible from here so I have devised a method for finding it.   Follow me.   Bear right, on a faint path, to the corner of the fenced wood over on the right where it meets the drive.   Standing at the corner, you will see that a shallow, grassy ditch crosses the grass opposite.   (If you look into the wood, you will see that it came from there before the drive was laid across it).   Cross the drive and follow the ditch between the avenue trees down to the low fence where you will find the stile that you need.   Climb over the twin-stiled, concrete footbridge and emerge into the uphill field on the other side. (There are Footpath arrows on the reverse of these stiles).

Bear right towards the unmarked first gate in the hedge and go through into the next uphill field.   Follow the left banked and oak-lined hedge up the ever steeper slope to the top of the field where you will find a gate in the far left corner.

Go through the gate with a Footpath pointer on the other side.   Carefully cross over the busy A37 Dorchester to Yeovil road and bear left towards 'The Rest and Welcome Inn.   In the area to the right of the inn, you will find two gates.   Go through the right gate with an angled 'Footpath' signpost.   The Footpath-arrowed exit stile on the other side of the field is about 100 yards to the left along the far wire fence, well down from the end of Brickyard Copse facing you (110º ESE). *The Footpath will not be clear so, if it looks difficult, you could walk anti-clockwise around the edge of the field until you pass the farm gate at the bottom end of the wire fence.   You would then find the Footpath-arrowed stile about 15 yards down in the right hedge.*   A double-sleeper bridge spans the stream which runs along the other side of the hedge and it is slippery when wet so be careful. On the other side of the ditch, go over another stile into the wet meadow.

In this meadow, there is a banked hedge running alongside the stream on your right and a long wood over on your left.   Start off by aiming for the far left end of the narrow strip of wood and you will go up a long ridge which runs along the field on your way.   Ignore the Footpath-arrowed stile in the left trees on your way. When you reach the far corner of the trees and the field widens to your left, keep walking until you find a farm gate in the adjacent hedge, down on the left.   Go through the gate where you will find a Footpath arrow on a post *on the other side*. Bear right for 100 yards to a Footpath-arrowed stile in the banked right hedge, just before a cattle trough.   Go over the stile and walk across to the first gate in the hedge on your left.

Out of the gate with a Footpath arrow on the other side, turn right onto the lane and then turn left down the lane signed for 'Church Farm'.   There are barns, sheds and entrances on the left as you begin to descend.   When the hedges give way to wire fences, you will see Church Farmhouse and the tiny stone church of St Edwold below you.   Well before the farmhouse, turn left through the gate marked 'To the Church' onto a right-curving track through the field.

96

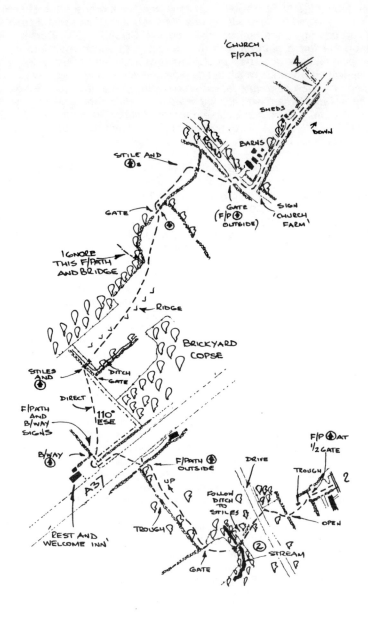

ROUTE 1 - STAGE 4

CHURCH FARM TO BUBB DOWN PLANTATION

Past the footbridge to St Edwold's church, your track crosses the stream and bears left.   The old track heads up to a fence-enclosed area with a small brick building inside but, as the notice says, 'Footpath Closed'.   The Dorset Council arrows on the fence point you to the correct path which runs into a mixed coppice, pine and oak wood by a Footpath-arrowed stile and a farm gate.   Follow the ascending chalky track which bends right and left through the woods.   *Here, Janet and I became honorary Jack Russells for a whole hour because we were joined by two little terriers who accompanied us up Bubb Down Hill and into Bubb Down Plantation.   They didn't come down to Melbury Bubb because it was too muddy for their little legs.   Sadly, we had to send them home because we were going to cross the A37 and were worried about their safety.*

At the top of this track you emerge onto Bubb Down Hill by another stile and gate. The yellow arrow points straight up the bowl of the hill with a ridge on your right. To find the 500ft O.S. trig. point, walk up the clear, easiest path around the bowl, rising and bearing left on the way up.   From the trig. point, you can go down to see the hamlet of Melbury Bubb or turn right and follow a rising line to **Point ***. It's only 1/4 mile down to Melbury Bubb and the lovely little church of St Mary the Virgin so it's well worth the detour and this is a meander after all.

So, bearing towards the fence on your left, you will find a Bridleway arrow on the fence-post.   Follow the left fence to a gate in the shady corner.   Through the gate, follow the direction of the Bridleway arrow - straight across the sloping field to walk anti-clockwise around the small brick building in the middle of the field.   It would be quicker to go straight down the field but the other way is the route on the Definitive Map.   So go round the shed and then head down the hill to the gate by the Dutch barn.   Through the gate, keep straight on down to the next gate and then follow the farm track alongside the stone wall which surrounds the fine mullioned Manor House.   Follow the lane round to the right into a wide area with the white gate of the churchyard facing you and with the road down on your left.

Go through the gate for your visit to the Church of St Mary the Virgin.   *When you see its old solid fuel heater with its fireguard and coal scuttles inside the door - together with its oil wall lights - you'll feel as if you've stepped back a few years. Bubb Down derives its name from Bubba, a Saxon who lived here, and the upside down font in the church was probably once the base of an Anglo-Saxon cross, so a church was here even then.   The church was rebuilt in 1474 and the tower from that date was retained when the church was again rebuilt in 1854.*

After your visit, retrace you steps up to the gate into the O S plinth field.   Then bear left across the rising hill to a gate in the wire fence **Point *** which leads into Stock Wood.   *Not the top corner gate - the one lower down.*   Follow the track, with a bank on your left and a deep valley on your right, to a gate onto a track which runs down to the A37.   Don't go down the track.   Execute a left hairpin and walk **up** the track to a wide grassy area on the right.   Turn right and follow the lower track through Bubb Down Plantation with a strip of wood and a field between you and the parallel A37 on your right.

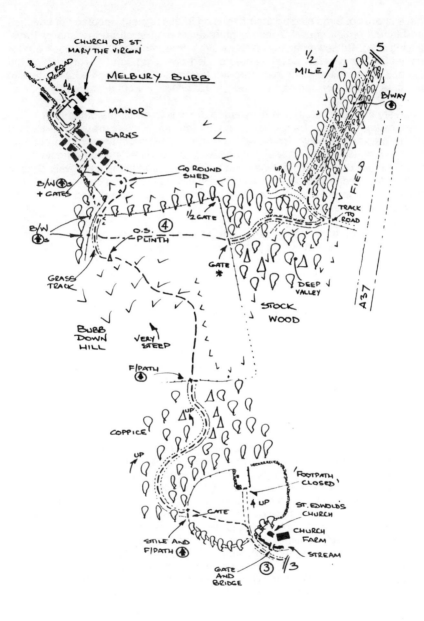

CHURCH OF ST. MARY THE VIRGIN

MELBURY BUBB

MANOR

BARNS

B/W + GATES

GO ROUND SHED

B/W

O.S. ④ PLINTH

½ GATE

GRASS TRACK

GATE *

DEEP VALLEY

STOCK WOOD

BUBB DOWN HILL

VERY STEEP

F/PATH

COPPICE

UP

UP

UP

FOOTPATH CLOSED

ST. EDWOLD'S CHURCH

CHURCH FARM

STREAM

GATE

STILE AND F/PATH

GATE AND BRIDGE

③ //3

½ MILE

B/WAY

FIELD

TRACK TO ROAD

A37

5

99

ROUTE 1 - STAGE 5

BUBB DOWN PLANTATION TO EVERSHOT

With a chorus of birds singing their heads off in this ancient woodland of beeches and birches, enjoy your 1/2 mile slightly ascending stroll on the chalky track, passing a left Bridleway arrow on the way. In another 200 yards, look out for another Bridleway-arrow post just before a left-sweeping bend. Turn right at the post and descend the steep path through the trees. You reach a half-gate with fine views to Melbury Sampford house. This brings you out onto the A37.

Very, very carefully cross over the road to the milestone on the other side. The gated, cattle-gridded entrance down on your left is to 'Hazel Farm'. The track is offered as a 'Permissive Bridleway' but the definitive Bridleway Number 9 is shorter - if un-signposted. Make your way through the little wood (directly away from the road) down to a small gate in the fence. Through the gate, walk straight on down the field to a large oak tree which stands alone on the corner of the track around the edge of Hazel Wood. Arriving at the oak, you will find a Bridleway arrow on the fence post.

Follow the gravel track alongside the fenced and ditched edge of the old wood on your left. Go through the Bridleway-arrowed gate onto the enclosed track with a wide verge on your right. Keep straight on, past the 'Private' half-gate into the woods opposite a gate in the right fence and then past a gated entrance into the woods opposite a stile and horse-jump in the right fence.

The track now bends right with a dark pine wood on the right and with old oaks on the left. After a gate into the left, hedged meadow, there are ditches on both sides which run down to join the stream which comes down the ancient oak-filled meadow and runs away into the wood on your right. The oaks near the stream are cloaked in lovely ferns. Rising up out of the valley, the track bends left whilst a more recent track now turns right for a new route on a - as the sign says - 'B/way to Mel. Osm.' Turn left and walk up the long, ascending track with the meadow over the hedge on your left. There is always a mixed wood on your right and you will soon have a deep, dark, pine wood on the left.

Keep on up, past a gate into the pasture on your left. The woods on the right begin to thin out and there are several pines scattered along the right ditch as you reach a cross-roads of tracks. There is a gate and on the wide left corner as the grassier left track is signed 'No Public Right of Way'. The right track continues through the woods but you keep straight on up. Two tracks run into the left woods as you continue past two water tanks on the right. Just past the tanks, the grass-verged track begins to descend. After a gate into both left and right fields, the track becomes deeper with harts-tongue ferns in the shady sides and oaks scattered along the high banks. Just past a huge old beech tree on the left, a driveway turns into a cottage on your left and the track now becomes tarmac with lower banks until you reconnect with the estate road from your starting point at the foot of Evershot hill.

This is where I showed you the junction with the Melbury Park drive on your way out, so turn left and it's not far back to the start........Off you go!

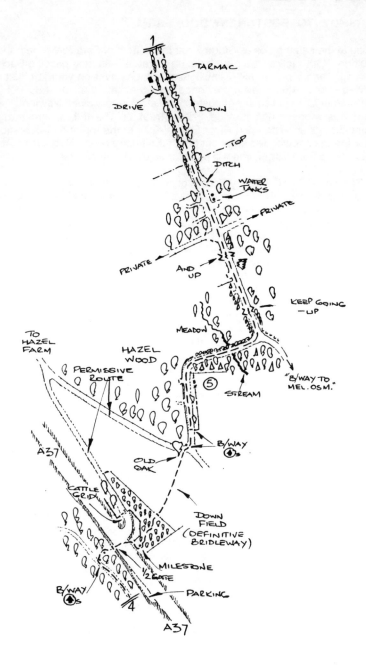

ROUTE 2 - STAGE 1

EVERSHOT TO FORTUNESWOOD FARM

Starting at the same place as Stage 1 - at the bottom of Fore Street near the drive to Melbury Park - follow the road back up towards Evershot, passing Back Lane on the right and a pair of stone-mullioned cottages over on your left, just before the Village Hall. After a few more cottages on the right, turn left at School Corner onto Summer Lane which is signposted 'Cattistock and Maiden Newton'. School Corner bus stop stands just up Fore Street on the left, where the raised pavement begins. The main River Frome rises at the top end of Evershot at St John's spring on a wooded ridge but another tributary rises at Holywell. Actually, if you walk up Fore Street, you will pass, or enjoy The Acorn Inn.

Past Sticklands C of E Primary School on your left and The Rectory on your right, the road bends right whilst ascending slightly. On the bend, nearly opposite the entrance to Summer Lodge Country House, go through the Footpath-arrowed gate in the left hedge into the sloping field. There are fine patchwork field views along the valley from here but these get better and better as you progress through this charming landscape. *According to Monica Hutchings in 'Inside Dorset' this is.....'typically Dorset, almost I might say (to the possible comment 'what again?') Dorset at its best'.* Now, get your bearings. Turn up the sloping field, aiming for the gap at the left end of the top hedge. On the way up, the gap becomes clearer and, when you arrive, you will find a Macmillan Way Footpath arrow pointing your way along the high slope.

Keep following the right hedge down, past a track which turns up into the top field (with West Woods Farm over the right horizon) and past a trough by an opening in the hedge. Approaching a clump of trees on your left, the views are even better as the field levels out and, after a right gate, you reach the end corner gate with another Macmillan Way arrow. Through this gate, aim for a spot about 100 yards to the left of the single oak tree on the other side of this wide field (only slightly left of straight on), passing a clump of oaks on your left on the way. You will find another Macmillan Way arrow at the partially hidden farm gate as you leave the field and join a tarmac lane running down from right to left.

Turn left down the lane between the left verged hedge and the right fenced field, following the descending drive into a pleasant area shaded with old oaks, now between fences, until a turning runs down into the yard and barns of Fortuneswood Farm. Stay on the main track, past the farmhouse and a row of cottages on your left. The track now climbs up, past another cottage on the right corner and along high banks to right and left, past a left turning track by a single large oak and up to a right bend into more barns. Don't follow the right bend but bear left here to join another track which runs along the left wire fence to lead you around to the left side of the large Dutch barn. Go through the gate with a Macmillan Way arrow on an adjacent post, where another track comes up from your left, and follow the main track straight across with a hedge on its right and a fence on its left.

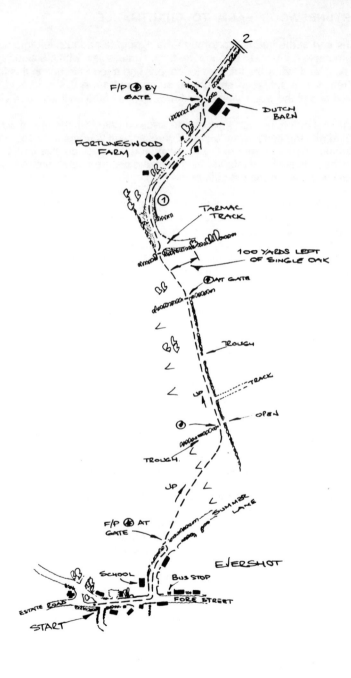

ROUTE 2 - STAGE 2

FORTUNESWOOD FARM TO CHANTMARLE

At the end of the hedge, go through the right gate and turn left into an area with innumerable gates. Go through the facing gate, again with a Macmillan arrow on the post, and follow the left wire fence, passing a round trough in this field. When the fence runs out, keep straight on across and down this wide field, aiming for the left end of the wood lying in the lower slopes of the field ahead of you.

At the foot of the field, go through the arrowed gate with the mixed wood on your left and with the hedge wandering off drunkenly on your right. Keep on down and cross the dry river valley to the gateway and the arrowed stile in the wire fence. From here, look ahead into the next field and picture a route between the last two electricity poles on the left side of the field.

Follow this route to the end of the left hedge where it turns sharp left onto a grass track. A single old oak stands on your right as the track continues right, in a grassy gully with a beech wood on its left. Pass close to the left of the oak and walk about 30 yards left along the facing hedge. Go over the stile in the banked hedge into a field which served as a football pitch for the Police Training College. Aim for the far left corner of the field (or pitch) into the beech trees. Go down the path between the trees with garages over on your right and join the descending grass track from your left. The track now has a high left bank and a right ditch as you meet the tarmac drive with a confirmation Bridleway signpost for 'Holway Farm 1' on the right corner.

The array of buildings once housed the Chantmarle Police Training College but it is now Octagon Village. As you follow the drive past the tree shaded lawns and parking areas on your left, the older sandstone building at the far end on your right is the original Chantmarle House. *In AD 1211, the 12th year of the reign of King John, Robert Chantmarle held lands here and these were later owned by John Chantmarle whose father had, through marriage, gained Bindon Abbey lands (not far from Wareham). In order to unencumber mortgages which had been raised on Chantmarle, it was sold to John Strode in 1596. It was he who added the superb 'new' house to the original 15thC building around 1606-12. He then began to build a private chapel which was completed in 1617.*

Strolling down the drive, admire the house and gardens and, if possible, glance unobtrusively over the wall just down past the ornate gates and you'll see the decorative moat, just before the sunken gardens over the fence on your right. Below you, you can see the River Frome threading its way through the gardens and under the embankment of the Dorchester to Yeovil railway line. As you cross the rail bridge, with a field on your left and Scots pines on your right, the banked drive ahead is a mass of daffodils at the right time of the year.

Before the banks with the iron fences, turn left through the first Footpath-arrowed gate onto the golf course. On a right bearing from the gate, there is a gable end of a cottage visible above the horizon. Aim right of this cottage and, as you progress across the course, you will see a stile in the facing hedge, next to a holly tree. Go over the arrowed stile into the next field which houses foundations of some old demolished buildings.

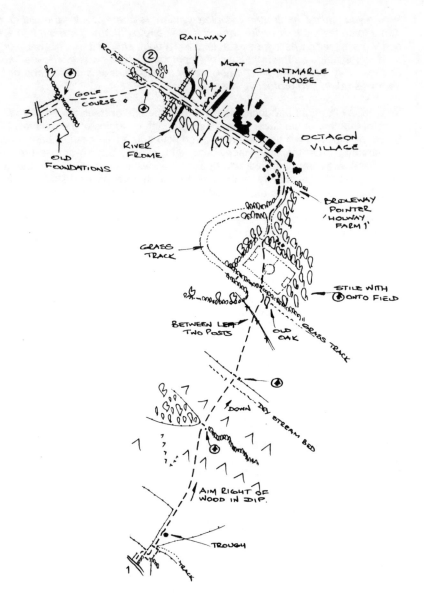

RAILWAY

②

ROAD

MOAT

CHANTMARLE HOUSE

GOLF COURSE

3

OLD FOUNDATIONS

RIVER FROME

OCTAGON VILLAGE

BRIDLEWAY POINTER 'HOLWAY FARM 1'

GRASS TRACK

STILE WITH ④ ONTO FIELD

BETWEEN LEFT TWO POSTS

OLD OAK

GRASS TRACK

④

DOWN DRY STREAM BED

④

AIM RIGHT OF WOOD IN DIP.

TROUGH

1

TRACK

ROUTE 2 - STAGE 3

CHANTMARLE TO FROME ST QUINTIN

Before you leave Chantmarle completely, there is a tale of a local poacher who, with a torch lashed to his rifle, chased a deer one night until it ran out into a wide open, grassy area where he was able to get a good shot at it.   This wide, grassy area turned out to be the front lawn of Chantmarle when it was the Police Training College.   My informant didn't say whether the poacher was prosecuted or if the deer was taken into protective custody.

Now, follow the right paddock fence down to the line of trees ahead of you. Yet another tributary of the River Frome runs along the margins of the next few fields. Down the dip, you will find an un-arrowed stile and a twin-sleeper bridge across the stream.   On the other side, bear right, slightly uppish across the marsh grass and away from the riverside trees.   You will find an opening in the hedge next to a wooden electricity gantry.   Go through onto the next sloping field and keep high up to brush the top left hedge as it bears round to the left.

Go over the stile in the top hedge and turn right to the half-gate in the next hedge (this is halfway down from the top hedge in this field).   There are farm buildings and a pond down on your right.   In this last field, keep straight on down towards the gate in the far left corner .

Through the gate, you will find a Footpath arrow on the far side.   You have arrived in Frome St Quintin.   *In the Domesday Book as Litel Frome held by the King, the St Quintin part comes from ancient lords of this manor.*   Turn left up the road. There is a steeply banked area of trees behind the ivy-clad stone wall on the left bend whilst there are a couple of houses on your right.   Then a track turns off right to a cottage on the bend and, immediately after that, a signed grass track leads, between the high left bank and wooden fence and a right stone wall, to a gate at its end.   To visit the little church go through the gate and up the field.

St Mary's dates back to the 12thC and the tower is probably Norman as it has a Norman doorway from the nave.   The stone and flint church has additions of the 14thC and 15thC but Hutchins says 'it is a small ancient building and contains nothing remarkable'.   Maybe oil wall lights weren't remarkable in Hutchins' time but they are now.   The site is lovely with its bird song and its bench in a sunny spot near the tower from which there are fine views of the village and the fields - if the hedge has been cut recently.

Two items struck me as worthy of mention.   First, in 1682 Sara Maber married one Thomas Hardy in St Mary's. No, not that Thomas Hardy.   No, not the Admiral, either.   Second, in the years between 1418 and 1511, there were nine rectors here, eight of whom were named William (the only other one was John Vagg, 1461-1487).

After your visit to St Mary's, return to the road and walk uphill.   At the top, there is a long brick wall on your right, shielding the gardens of the 1782 Manor House. You can glimpse the gracious brick and stone building through the ornate gates half way along.   Keep straight on for 1/2 mile, descending and ascending again past cottages and banked hedges to fields on either side.

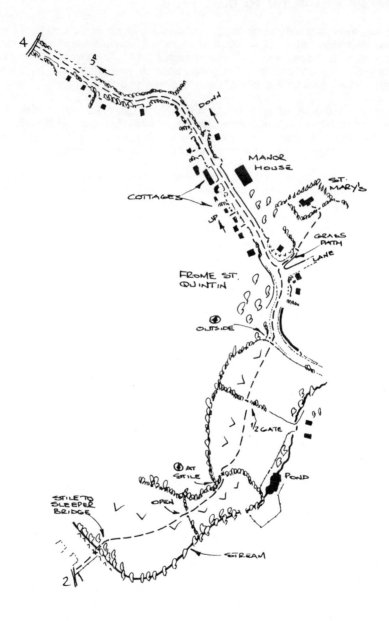

ROUTE 2 - STAGE 4

FROME ST QUINTIN TO BURL FARM

Soon, there is a wide verge on the left and you arrive at a crossing of tracks as the road bends right. The signpost on the right island confirms directions along the tracks to 'Yeovil Road 1/2' and 'Evershot 1.1/2'. We're on our way back to Evershot now so turn down the gravel track on your left but not before looking over the left gate for a lovely retrospective view of Chantmarle.

Enjoying the downhill stroll, the farm which you can see on the slopes ahead of you is Burl Farm, your next immediate target, whilst you can see the West Woods Farm ridge over on your left. After a low left ditch, at a low part of the track with a gate in the right hedge, another grassy track turns down left through a gate.

Now, go up and over a ridge on your rutted, grassy track and you will soon arrive at an abandoned, ivy-clad cottage on your right with a clump of trees on your left. This is Ladymead Cottage. Go through the gate into the downhill field and keep straight on, avoiding the electricity pole's support cable en route. In the bottom right corner, go over the stile onto the approach to the Yeovil-Dorchester rail track and, as the notice says, 'Stop, Look, Listen - Beware of Trains'. If all clear, quickly cross the track into the safety of the narrow, fenced enclosure on the other side and go down to another stile into the wooded valley bottom with the young River Frome threading its way from Holywell. Cross the stream where it flows under an oak tree and negotiate the marshy bottom edge of this next uphill field, passing roots and plants of wild iris on the way up. Don't wander off the narrow path or you might fall into one of the low water tanks.

In high summer, the irises, horsetails and nettles are sometimes neglected and left uncut and the path is impossible to find. The exit from this field is in the top right corner and, if you are properly dressed, crash your way through whilst keeping about 2 yards from the right ditch. This will keep you safe from other wet ditches or the ponds hidden over to the left.

At the top of the field, go through the Footpath-arrowed half-gate in the right fence and wander along the top left slope to find your way to the stile in the wire fence.

I have had to report problems with the next stage of the Footpath through Burl Farm to Dorset Council because various obstructions have been built across the Path on the Frome St Quintin to Evershot section - including a banked slurry pit.

The route shown in this book is the nearest possible to the official Footpath and has been walked by hundreds of readers of the first 'Circular Dorset Rambles' book since 1996. Over the stile, bear left and cross to the fence around the banked slurry pit. Follow the fence clockwise and up to the second gate (the first leads into the slurry pit). Through the gate, turn sharp left before the barn and walk up the steep field to pass close left of a clump of trees. Now, pass right of another oak tree up on your left. Over the brow of the hill, you will see a hedge facing you with a trough and a gate close to an oak and a holly tree. Do not go through the second right gate. Go through the gate immediately right of the trough into the next field

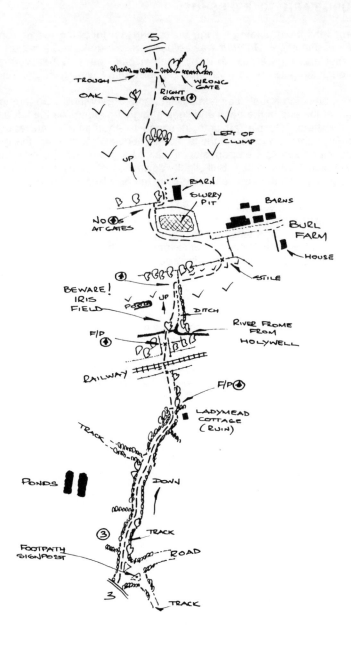

ROUTE 2 - STAGE 5

BURL FARM TO EVERSHOT

Cross this field, aiming for the far corner (not following the right hedge to the nearer corner).   On your way across, you will make out a trough near the top corner and a gate next to it, by another oak tree.   When you get there, go through the gate and turn left onto the track from Holywell via Burl Farm.

Now, all being equal, it's plain sailing back to Evershot.   Go through the facing gate at the end of the track and keep straight on alongside the left banked hedge in this field.   Past a left gate, descend to another left gate and a Footpath-arrowed gate facing you in the far corner hedge.   Go through this gate and keep straight on across the open, sloping field to a gap in the opposite banked hedge, just below a short oak.   Still slightly downhill, walk straight across to an oak tree and go through the arrowed half-gate in the next hedge and fence.

In this last field, you will see a single oak tree ahead of you and clumps of bushes and trees running along the bottom left of the sloping field.   Turn half down the slope and aim for a stile next to a holly tree.   On the way down, for the correct Footpath line, you shouldn't come any closer than 30 yards to that oak tree.   *If the field has been planted with sweetcorn or anything else impassable, take a clockwise path around the edge.*   Arriving at the Footpath-arrowed stile, go over it and up and over a bushed bank to drop down to a stream.   Yes, the young River Frome again arriving from St John's Well.   Cross the stream by the simple bridge and go up and over another bank to cross a ditch, finally ascending to the tarmac track with rough common on the other side.   Turn right onto the track and follow it alongside the hazel and willow clad stream, past a gate where the stream runs under the track and into an open area where there is a thatched stable block and some garages.   *On the other side of the stream, now on your left, is the old Common Farm - or rather was the old Common Farm as plans were being considered in 1996 for the building of 21 dwellings.   There may be 21 dwellings on the other side of the stream.   Anyway, I think that covers all possibilities so a further revision to 'The Melbury Meander' shouldn't be necessary just yet.*

Anyway, keep following the track into 'The Common' and emerge close to your shared starting point with Route 1 - Stage 1 and with The Acorn Inn awaiting you up the hill to your left.

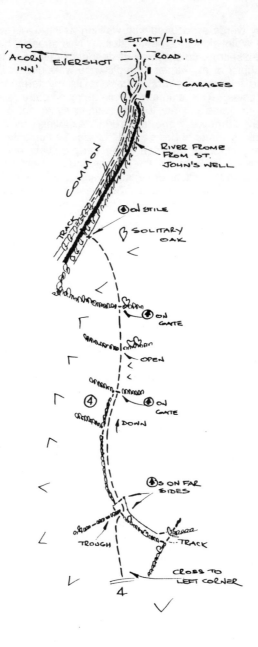

START/FINISH

TO 'ACORN INN'   EVERSHOT   ROAD.

GARAGES

RIVER FROME FROM ST. JOHN'S WELL

COMMON

TRACK

ON STILE

SOLITARY OAK

ON GATE

OPEN

④

ON GATE

DOWN

S ON FAR SIDES

TROUGH   TRACK

CROSS TO LEFT CORNER

4

PART SIX- THE BOTTLEBUSH ROUND

INTRODUCTION

I couldn't find any words associated with walking which begin with a B so I've used one of A.W.Wainwright's favourite titles.   This strange, tumuli-bedecked and Roman road-bisected, upland area of deepest Dorset has long fascinated me.   It is the subject of my earlier long-distance walk guide *'The Cranborne Chase Path'* and I have been drawn back to its mysterious footpaths and bridleways many times.   This is an ancient forest, much patronised by Royalty in Tudor and Jacobean times and this, together with its avoidance by the builders of the Great Western Turnpike in the late 18thC, explains why it has remained undeveloped.   This is a land of Bronze and Iron-age settlements and it has been the scene of many conflicts between these early settlers and the hordes of invaders who included the Romans, the Saxons and the Normans.   Since then, there have been many conflicts on a lesser scale, although no less bloody, between poachers and Chase wardens.   So, breathe in the atmosphere and *go quietly!*   You never know what you might see if you travel circumspectly.

Parking is available at Squirrels Corner, at many places along the wide verges of the B3081 and in Cranborne Square.   You can't really get a bus to Squirrels Corner but Wilts and Dorset buses 184 and 185 will deliver you from Dorchester, Blandford or Salisbury to Handley Cross roundabout just 1/2 mile away.   There are also Rural Buses to Cranborne village including Nos. 41, 300 and 303.

The alternative Routes, which are mostly along easy farm tracks and paths, all begin with the shortest walk so that extensions from it are easier to follow and, when you turn off to the longer alternatives, I will tell you what you can expect to come across along the way.   Of course, whichever option you choose, you won't cover all of the sections in one day so, when you fall under the spell of Cranborne Chase, you can come back and enjoy all of the other Routes.

Because 'undeveloped', Cranborne Chase doesn't have all of the usual facilities, although Cranborne itself boasts two fine inns and a good shop/post office - and there is a handy petrol station on the A354 just off the end of the Ackling `Dyke on Routes 1, 2 and 3.   So pack a good lunch in your backpack, lace up your walking boots and go and have a fine day's hiking over some of the best chalk downs and farmland anywhere in the County - or even in the whole country.

THE ALTERNATIVES

Starting in the parking area amongst the trees at Squirrels Corner on the B3081 (Reference SU025153 on O S Map No. 184), these round walks cover between 5.1/4 and 13.1/2 miles, depending on which option you choose.   Routes 1,2 and 4 all begin at Route 1 - Stage 1.   Route 3 has its own start map called Route 3 - Stage 1.   Oh, and O S Map No. 195 may come in handy as well.

ROUTE 1: Total distance 5.1/4 miles - This shortest of the four walks takes you along the Roman Ackling Dyke to a unique series of tumuli, up to Penbury Knoll hill fort, past the source of the River Crane and back to Squirrels Corner along some fine tracks and a Drove Road, field footpaths and open downland.

ROUTE 2: Total distance 7.1/2 miles - The extra miles added to Route 1 take you all the way into Cranborne where you can visit the Manor House gardens and the Church and learn something of the history of the centre of this Royal Chase.

ROUTE 3: Total distance 5.1/4 miles - This is the Route with its own start map (Route 3 - Stage 1) and it takes you to the South of the B3081. The route includes a fine walk along farm tracks, through woodlands, across the Monkton-up-Wimborne road and over the River Allen to Harley Wood. It includes a mysterious and shady stretch of the Ackling Dyke and it can be added conveniently to any of the other Routes to make an interesting extension.

ROUTE 4: Total distance 12.3/4 miles - This 'ultimate' Route is formed from the outer edge of the whole circuit to make the longest possible alternative. By following Route 2, you will arrive back at Squirrels Corner after 7.1/2 glorious miles and then you can carry on with Route 3 for another 5.1/4 miles. This way, - after a refuelling stop at Squirrels Corner - you get to see the best of the area all at once.

STAGE	MILES	TOTAL MILES
ROUTE 1:		
1.1 Squirrels Corner start	0	0
1.2 Squirrels Corner to Ackling Dyke	1.25	1.25
1.3 Ackling Dyke to Cursus Gate	1	2.25
1.4 Cursus Gate to Pentridge Hill	.75	3
1.5 Pentridge Hill to Bowldish Pond	1.50	4.50
1.1 Bowldish Pond to Squirrels Corner	.75	**5.25**
ROUTE 2:		
To Pentridge Hill as Route 1 - Stages 1 to 4	3	3
1.5 Pentridge Hill to Drove Road	.75	3.75
3.1 Drove Road to Cranborne Manor	1.25	5
3.2 Cranborne Manor to Cranborne Dairy Farm	1.25	6.25
3.3 Cranborne Dairy Farm to B3081	1	7.25
1.1 B3081 to Squirrels Corner	.25	**7.50**

STAGE	MILES	TOTAL MILES
ROUTE 3:		
3.1 Squirrels Corner to Monkton Up Wimborne	1.25	1.25
3.2 Monkton Up Wimborne to Harley Wood	1.25	2.50
3.3 Harley Wood to Bottlebush Down	1.75	4.25
To Squirrels Corner on Route 1 - Stages 2 and 1	1	**5.25**
ROUTE 4:		
Route 2 all the way round and back plus Route 3 all the way out and back		**12.75**

Ackling Dyke stile, Bottlebush Down. Page 118

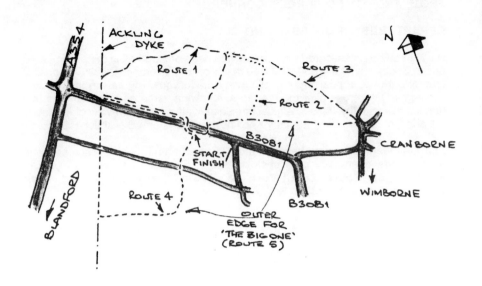

Cranborne Manor House. Page 128

ROUTE 1 - STAGE 1

FROM AND TO SQUIRRELS CORNER

DEPARTURES - ROUTES 1 AND 2:

Having parked and secured your car, having been dropped off in the parking area on the South side of the B3081 at Squirrels Corner (Reference SU025153 on O S Map No. 184 to repeat myself) or having made your way here from Handley Cross, carefully cross over the road to a very wide verge on the other side and turn left between the trees.   Almost immediately, there is a fine view of Pentridge Hill and the earthworks of Penbury Knoll beyond the nearer Blackbush Hill.

That's all there is for now because most of the Stage 1 map is concerned with making sure everybody gets back safely.   **So, whether you are doing Route 1 or Route 2, all turn to Route 1 - Stage 2 and keep following Route 1 until I tell you.**

RETURNING - CHOOSE YOUR ROUTE NUMBER AND READ ON:

ROUTE 1 - BOWLDISH POND TO SQUIRRELS CORNER

Keep following the track down with the open field on your right and with a gate in the bushes on your left, just before an open area with Bowldish Pond beyond some scrubby bushes on your left.   If you keep close to the edge of the embankment on your right, you will come to a brick footbridge, between trees, over a small stream.   This is preferred because the main track descends into a ford across the upper reaches of the River Crane which can be particularly boggy after wet weather.

Now, emerging from the trees with footpath arrows on the right corner post, you meet a junction of tracks.   Keep straight on up the chalk and flint track to a conglomeration of gates at the top.   You meet the Route 2 walkers here.   Now read on :

ROUTES 1 AND 2 - ARRIVING AT B3081 TOGETHER:

You all arrive at a collection of gates and a stile onto the B3081.   Carefully cross over the road to the high grass verge on the other side and turn right.   There is a field at first behind the hedge on your left but this soon gives way to a mixed pine and deciduous wood.   The views over the fields on your right are extensive and you can see back to where you reached the Cursus gate earlier today.

Keep on the verge, past a wooden barrier with a 'Private. Keep Out' sign in the woods, until you arrive back at the entrance to the car parking area.

Now try Route 3   It will take you South into completely different country where you will hear of a strange happening and a local prediction of Armageddon.

ROUTE 3 - ARRIVALS: Just cross over.   You're back.

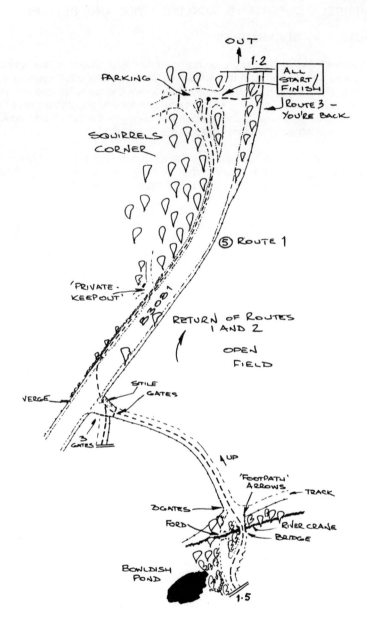

ROUTE 1 - STAGE 2

SQUIRRELS CORNER TO ACKLING DYKE AND RETURN

ROUTE 1 - DEPARTURES:

As you walk along this very wide verge, under and around a fine row of beech trees, you should find that the grass has been mowed quite short and there is ample parking along a very long stretch between the roadside and the wire fence on your right.   After a pair of stump-protected tumuli, one either side of the road (or was it a long barrow, sliced through the middle?), the long bank running away over on your left is one of two edges of the Dorset Cursus.

On your right, an opening in the fence at the junction of two fields gives a view of the continuing line of the Cursus which actually runs along the right edge of the wood which you can see at the end of the descending wire fence.

The Dorset Cursus was a ceremonial route of indeterminate origin with parallel banks about 1/4 mile apart.   It strides across Bottlebush Down from Gussage Hill to Martin Down - although little is visible from the ground.   The Romans cut straight across it with their Ackling Dyke about 1 mile South-West of here.   In much the same way, the Turnpike builders built over the Ackling Dyke down in the distance on your right where the Dyke runs into, and becomes, the A354.

Anyway, keep straight on and you will soon arrive at a solitary crab-apple tree and a footpath-arrowed stile onto the top of the Roman Ackling Dyke on your right.   Climb over the stile and follow the faint path as it zig-zags through some sparse hawthorn bushes on a descending slope. Down on your right, there is a grassy track which you can use if the Dyke is overgrown.   In about 400 yards, at a cutting, come down off the Dyke and join the bottom track along the field edge.

ROUTE 3 - ARRIVALS:

Cross over the A354 and turn right.   Follow the wide verge for about 1/2 mile until you are almost back at the parking area where you began.   Then turn to Route 1 - Stage 1 again.

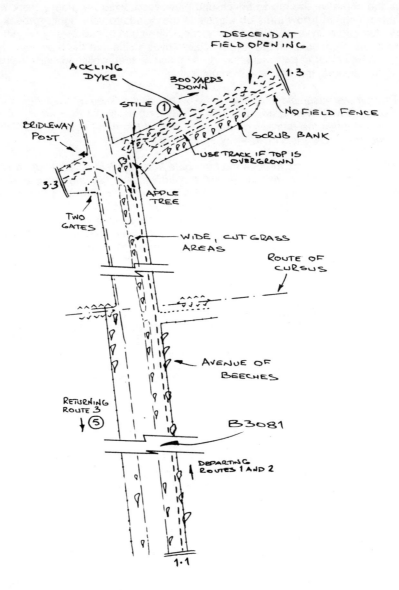

DESCEND AT
FIELD OPENING

ACKLING
DYKE

300 YARDS
DOWN

1·3

STILE ①

NO FIELD FENCE

BRIDLEWAY
POST

SCRUB BANK

USE TRACK IF TOP IS
OVERGROWN

3·3

APPLE
TREE

TWO
GATES

WIDE, CUT GRASS
AREAS

ROUTE OF
CURSUS

AVENUE OF
BEECHES

RETURNING
ROUTE 3
↓ ⑤

B3081

DEPARTING
ROUTES 1 AND 2

1·1

119

ROUTE 1 - STAGE 3

ACKLING DYKE TO CURSUS GATE

At the corner of the mixed beech and pine wood, where a grassy track with a faded footpath arrow turns off alongside the woods to your right, go back onto the top of the Dyke.   After a few yards, with vague tracks nearby on your left, next to a horse-jump in the wire fence, go over a stile into the next field. Here, tumuli and other earthworks abound - so much so that, whilst adjoining fields are always planted, this field is left untouched.

This famous assemblage of disc and bowl barrows is listed by L V Grinsell under 'Oakley Down, Wimborne St Giles - the finest barrows of their kind'.   Oakley Down includes the barrows on the other side of the A354 over on your left and Wimborne St Giles is 3 miles away South-East from here.

Where a track comes through the farm gate from the field on your right and cuts across your path to disappear into the tumuli field, an intriguing earthwork presents itself.   Basically, it is a 216 ft diameter disc barrow with two tumps (internal mounds) inside it and with two cuttings through it.   In true road builders style, the Romans cut straight into the edge of this ancient monument rather than bend the Ackling Dyke a few feet.   As Heywood Sumner says in his 1913 treatise 'Both roads (this and the A354) cut into the barrow circles and both thus express a silent disregard for departed glory'.   When the barrows in this field were excavated in Victorian times, nearly every one contained a cremation urn, amber beads and some bronze artefacts.

Now, back on top of the Dyke, go over the stile next to the horse-jump into the next right field and follow the top of the Dyke for another 60 yards.   Go over the unmarked stile in the right wire fence which cuts diagonally across the Dyke and bear left to keep straight on along the top of the Dyke.   If the grass is long and the going is hard, come down into the field on your right and follow its edge, parallel with the Dyke.   Ignore the half-gate with a Bridleway arrow pointing into the rising field.

In little more than 100 yards, whether you are on top of or alongside the Dyke, you will reach the end of the field to find a Footpath-arrowed stile in the fence. A wide grassy Bridleway runs from left to right along your side of this wire fence. On your left, it leads to a petrol station which may have a few provisions for the rest of your walk but you must turn right here and follow the Bridleway up the edge of the field.   After a bit of a climb and an ensuing short descent, you arrive at a gateway into the next field.   This is a good spot to stop for a minute or two.

From here, there is a lovely view of Pentridge Hill, Penbury Knoll hill fort and the natural arena which lies within their curves.   Over on the left, there is a glimpse of the spire of St Rumbold's Church in Pentridge.

The section of wire fence on the right of the gate, together with the far edge of the Salisbury Plantation Wood, exactly follows the line of the Dorset Cursus.   As you go through the gateway to begin a descent into the next field, you cross its Eastern flank on the brow of this hill.

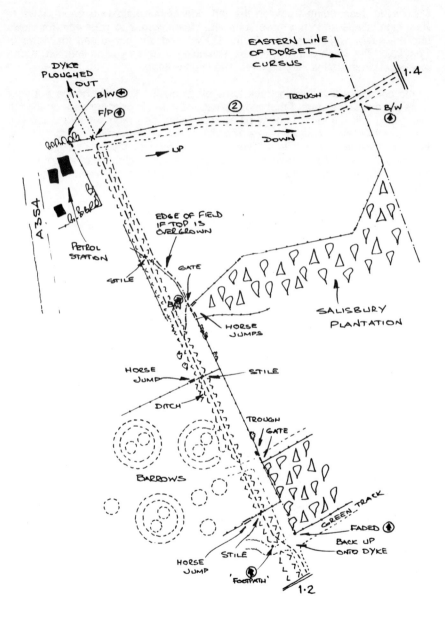

EASTERN LINE
OF DORSET
CURSUS

1·4

TROUGH

B/W

DYKE
PLOUGHED
OUT

B/W

F/P

②

DOWN

UP

A354

PETROL
STATION

EDGE OF FIELD
IF TOP IS
OVERGROWN

GATE

STILE

BM

HORSE
JUMPS

SALISBURY
PLANTATION

HORSE
JUMP

STILE

DITCH

TROUGH
GATE

BARROWS

GREEN TRACK

FADED

BACK UP
ONTO DYKE

HORSE
JUMP

STILE

'FOOTPATH'

1·2

CURSUS GATE TO PENTRIDGE HILL

Follow the descending track on the left side of this field with good views to Pentridge village and church on your left.   Look across to your right for views into the valley which leads up to the B3081 and straight ahead for views of Pentridge Hill - which you will soon be ascending.   Below you on your left, a long row of tall pines strides off on a direct line into Pentridge.

At the bottom of this field, a track turns off alongside the right hedge but your route goes past the start of that line of pines, past an old opening back on the left into a field and round to a boggy bit of track (unless it's high summer when you walk this Route).   *This is where the Pentridge village valley bottom drains towards the headwaters of the River Crane.   I hope it's dry and set hard when you arrive.*   After Bridleway arrows on a posts on your right, either side of a gate into the valley bottom, the track bears round to the left, between hedges, to Pentridge.

In the Domesday Book, Pentridge is listed as 'Pentric' - belonging to the Church of Glastonbury.   The name is derived from the British 'pen', a head or chief part and 'ridge', as of a hill.

But don't go to Pentridge today, though.   Turn right, through twin gates by the Bridleway arrow, and follow the uphill, deeply rutted track with grass up the middle, round a left bend with an open field on your right.

With the track less sunken for a while but then deeply eroded again, pass a horse-jump in the fence on your right and a few scrubby bushes on both sides. After much ascending, you will reach the last gate across the track.   Go through the gate onto the grazing slopes of the Hill where you will find tractor tracks fading into the grass.   *There are views on your right to the B3081 and beyond as far as Bulbarrow Hill.*   Keep on, following the fence on your right into and out of a dip, up to a farm gate and a half at the top end of the fence.

I know I said that Penbury Knoll hill fort was on this Route.   Well, it is, if you turn left here and wander over the top slopes of the hill, and through the small gate into the pine woods.   The slopes of the earthworks are clearly visible on the far side of Pentridge Hill and are well worth a picnic stop.   Come back to this small gate with Bridleway and Jubilee Trail arrows when you've finished exploring. There are two stones on its left.   One carries the Ordnance Survey benchmark for some unspecified height and the other bears a crown, the letter 'S' and the date '1891'.   Go through the gate into a wide, well horse-trodden area with trees on either side.

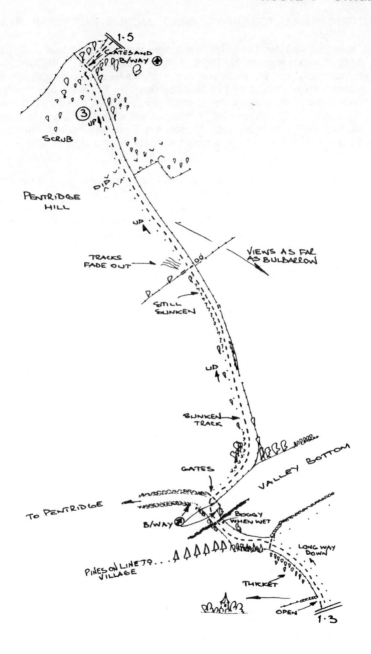

1·5

GATES AND
B/WAY

③

SCRUB

UP

PENTRIDGE
HILL

DIP

UP

TRACKS
FADE OUT

VIEWS AS FAR
AS BULBARROW

STILL
SUNKEN

UP

SUNKEN
TRACK

VALLEY BOTTOM

GATES

TO PENTRIDGE

B/WAY

BOGGY
WHEN WET

LONG WAY
DOWN

PINES ON LINE TO...
VILLAGE

THICKET

OPEN

1·3

123

ROUTE 1 - STAGE 5

PENTRIDGE HILL TO DROVE ROAD AND/OR BOWLDISH POND

Make sure that you don't bear off to the right here because that particular gate only leads to a gate marked 'No Right of Way. Please Keep to Bridleway'. Keep to the clear track, past the Bridleway arrow on the fence corner post (sometimes overgrown with brambles and/or blackberries).   Between banks, the track descends slightly with a hedge on your left, an open field on your right and grass up the middle.   Fine views begin to open out ahead as the Bridleway/track undulates gently.   After a good 1/4 mile, the Bridleway rises to meet a pair of farm gates either side of a Footpath-arrowed stile on your right.

AND NOW, IT'S DECISION TIME - DO YOU TAKE THE SHORTEST WAY BACK OR CARRY ON TO CRANBORNE?

We'll take the shorter Route 1 first and, when I've taken the Route 1 amblers past Bowldish Pond to Squirrels Corner, I'll come back and find you Route 2 walkers. Can't wait that long?   Oh, all right then.

ROUTE 2: TURN TO ROUTE 2 - STAGE 1

ROUTE 1:

Now, all of you Route 1 walkers, turn off the Bridleway here.   Over this stile, you are in a very long field, with a wire fence and a hedge on your right and a steady climb ahead of you.   Fortunately, there is a very wide, grassy path specially for you all the way up.   *Near the brow of the hill there are some distant objects to find with your compass.   At 144 º SE, you can just see the Isle of Wight,.   At 168 º SSE, you can see the flats on Bournemouth Overcliff and, at 184 º S, you can see the Purbeck hills.*

Over the brow of the hill, you soon reach the end of the field, with a wire fence facing you.   There is a farm gate on your right with a Footpath-arrowed stile on its post.   If you think about it, the arrows on both sides of this particular post point to exactly the wrong directions.   Anyway, go over the stile and immediately turn left onto a grassy farm track.   A repetition of the earlier 'No Right of Way' sign protects Blackbush Down which faces you at this gate.   Follow the track to the next fence with another stile and arrow.   Go over this next stile and join the downhill track around a couple of bends.

In the shade of the bushes at the side of this track, I once disturbed a fallow deer.   It's amazing how quickly they wake up.   He was away almost before I'd noticed him.   It takes me a lot longer than that to become active after I wake up.

Anyway, keep on down the footpath, with varying hedges, fences and hawthorns on your left, past a turning to a pair of farm gates at a bend on your left, and down to a small personnel gate with a Footpath arrow on it.   Through the gate, join the downward track, bearing left at first.   The right track is clearly signed again 'No Right Of Way'.   Now, turn back to Route 1 - Stage 1 for instructions on the last few hundred yards to Squirrels Corner.

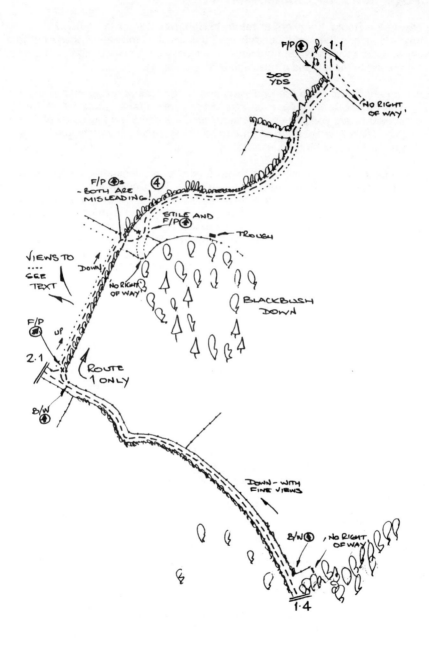

ROUTE 2 - STAGE 1

DROVE ROAD TO CRANBORNE

Leaving the Route 1 walkers to return to Squirrels Corner the quick way, keep straight on along the slightly undulating track which immediately opens out to a very wide area with hawthorn bushes in the grassy bank on your right. The track veers round to the left and drops slightly to a junction.

On the right corner there are Bridleway and Hardy Trail arrows pointing back the way you have come. *There is also a very comfortable grassy bank by the corner gate where you can sit and enjoy the views down into the valley of Toby's Bottom. There is a Footpath down through those fields beyond the gate on your left whilst a Footpath/Track turns off to your right .*

Keep straight on for quite a while, between the higher fenced field on your right and the hedge on a dipping fence on your left. The Bridleway rises a little and, after a higher patch and a single beech tree on the right, the track widens out and levels. The right fence gives way to a banked hedge and an entrance into the right field has been replaced by a 'Hampshire Gate'. This is a movable section of barbed-wire fence which, in Hampshire, they call a 'Dorset Gate'. As the right, banked hedge becomes infiltrated by holly bushes, the wide grassy track continues to rise slightly and you reach an opening into an old beech and ash wood on a low hill on the left.

Here, the track is not so wide and opposing openings lead into a left clearing and a right field which drops to the Crane valley. You now begin to descend as the banked track wends its way down. Just before a holly tree on the left, there is a sudden, brief view ahead of you to the Church of Saints Mary and Bartholomew in Cranborne. At a Bridleway-arrowed gate across the track, you pass around the left end onto tarmac. When a wide track emerges through a pair of gates on your right, there is a partial view ahead of Cranborne Manor House.

Still descending, with banked hedges either side, you arrive at a junction with the ancient Cranborne to Martin and Toyd Down road which once led all the way to Salisbury before being superseded by the Great Western Turnpike (the A354). The signpost on the corner verge indicates the ways to 'Boveridge 1.1/2 and Martin 4.3/4'. Keep to the right banked hedge with a row of trees on the left side of the road . In a few yards, before the '30' sign and the first house in Cranborne (for this is where you are), there is a 'Salisbury Street' plaque on the right brick wall. Turn right onto the path to the kissing gate at the top end with a field on your right and the tile-topped, rendered garden wall on your left.

Go through the gate and turn sharp left to keep the line of successive garden walls on your left. Aim for the right end of the cottages with the 'eyebrow' windows at the bottom of the field.

If it's the rainy season or any time in the winter, before you leave Cranborne, it might be a good idea to take a couple of plastic carrier bags with you ready for Stage 3. Have a quick look at the Stage 3 notes if you don't like surprises.

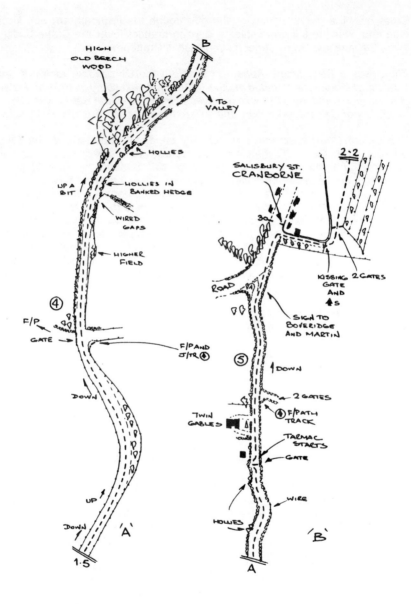

HIGH
OLD BEECH
WOOD

B

TO
VALLEY

HOLLIES

2·2

SALISBURY ST.
CRANBORNE

UP A
BIT

HOLLIES IN
BANKED HEDGE

WIRED
GAPS

30

HIGHER
FIELD

KISSING 2 GATES
GATE
AND
S

ROAD

SIGN TO
BOVERIDGE
AND MARTIN

④

F/P

GATE

F/P AND
J/TR ④

⑤

DOWN

2 GATES

④ F/PATH
TRACK

DOWN

TWIN
GABLES

TARMAC
STARTS

GATE

UP

WIRE

DOWN

'A'

HOLLIES

'B'

1·5

A

127

ROUTE 2 - STAGE 2

CRANBORNE TO CRANBORNE DAIRY FARM

Cross over the gravel driveway and go through the Footpath-arrowed kissing gate and over the following stile. Zig-zag right/left over the Crane bridge to follow the lane into Swan Street for your visit to Cranborne.

There was a Benedictine Abbey here before the Domesday Book but Abbot Giraldus of Cranborne founded another Abbey in Tewkesbury in 1091 and, eleven years later, he and the 57 monks removed there Cranborne Abbey was demoted to a Priory or Cell of Tewkesbury and so it remained until it was dissolved in 1540.

The Chase Court was held here, mainly because Robert Cecil, 1st Earl of Salisbury and Queen Elizabeth's First Secretary, later James I's Lord Treasurer, lived in Cranborne Manor House (as do his descendants to this day) and the Court was conveniently held there. Robert Cecil entertained James I on his many hunting trips and, after Cecil's death in 1612, James returned here many times between 1615 and 1623. Following damage to the house during the Civil War, when the Cecils supported Parliament, the house was unoccupied for many years but, after a 100 year period of use as farmhouses, it was renovated by the 2nd Earl of Salisbury in 1863 (the title of Earl of Salisbury having been extinct for many of the intervening years). Cranborne once enjoyed a prime position on the road from Poole to Salisbury but the Great Western Turnpike, which was begun in 1755, passed it by and Cranborne's importance was ended.

Now, leave The Square to the left of the shady, public garden into Swan Street whence you arrived, past the gates to the Church of Sts Mary and Bartholomew. *The main fabric of the church is of the 13th and 15th Century, with a 15thC tower and pulpit, but the North doorway dates back to the 12thC and there are 14thC wall paintings inside. The church was restored in 1875.*

Carry on to the end of Swan Street where the 'Strictly Private' drive leads into the grounds of the Manor House. Veer off right to the stile and across to the kissing gate in the wooden fence ahead of you. Through the gate, walk up to the gravel track , bearing left before passing through the avenue of beech trees that leads to the gardens of the Manor House. Now the track has gained a row of fence-protected trees along its left flank and a wire-fenced field on the right. After nearly 1/2 mile, go through the gate across the track at Manor Farm and join the tarmac lane straight on. There are brick farm buildings on your right and a lane goes off over the River Crane on the left. Past the poplars on the left corner, there is a wire fence and a hedge at the edge of the meadow and, after the cottage on your right, the lane bends slightly. After a wide entrance to the low field across the river on the left, keep straight on. Go past a wide track/Footpath on your right. Then pass a hidden, derelict barn in a hedged, abandoned orchard. Eventually, you reach two gates into the right field and pass through a pair of gates across your path. Now, with Cranborne Dairy Farm house and garden on your left, turn right, skirting round the storage tank on the near right corner. Go across to the small gate signed 'Please Shut the Gate' next to two corner field gates. Go through the Footpath gate or, if it the path is overgrown with nettles - as it sometimes is in high summer - go through the pair of gates instead and follow the left edge of the field, parallel with the path.

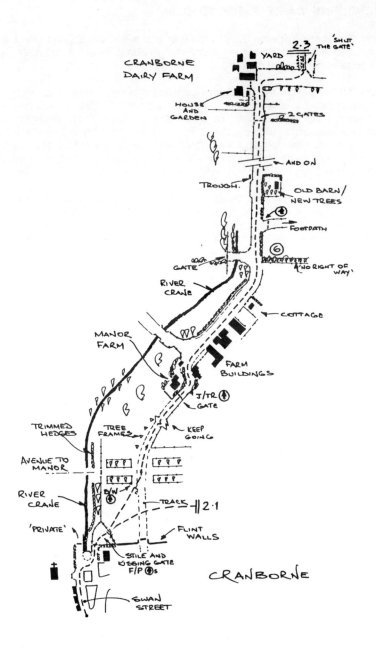

CRANBORNE
DAIRY FARM

YARD

2.3

'SHUT THE GATE'

HOUSE AND GARDEN

2 GATES

AND ON

TROUGH.

OLD BARN/ NEW TREES

FOOTPATH

GATE

6

'NO RIGHT OF WAY'

RIVER CRANE

COTTAGE

MANOR FARM

FARM BUILDINGS

J/TR GATE

TRIMMED HEDGES

TREE FRAMES

KEEP GOING

AVENUE TO MANOR

B/W

RIVER CRANE

TRACK 2.1

'PRIVATE'

FLINT WALLS

STILE AND KISSING GATE F/Ps

CRANBORNE

SWAN STREET

129

ROUTE 2 - STAGE 3

CRANBORNE DAIRY FARM TO B3081

Whether you are following the Footpath or you are in the adjacent field, there is an excavated farmyard down on your left.   In about 70 yards, the path - and the field edge - both lead to an iron gate.

Turn left through your own particular gate and you will all now keep encircling the yard which has become fenced-in as well as banked.   Past the left turn into the yard, signed 'No Right of Way', go over the stile next to the gates in the wooden fencing at the bottom of the track.   Turn left into the very wide area which is a mass of wooden fencing and farm gates with a wire fence bounding the field on your right.   Follow the wire fence round, with barns, silage tanks and outbuildings of Cranborne Dairy Farm on your left, dropping down to ford the River Crane.

This is where you need the plastic bags I mentioned in Cranborne because the stream can be deeper than it looks and the wire fence that crosses it won't support you.   After rain or during the winter season, the Crane runs clear and deep.   At other times, it practically dries up but then it becomes a pool of diluted cattle effluent.   *I dread to think what happens to the downstream habitat when the rains come and wash the bovine residues away.*   However, just slip the plastic bags over your boots and all will be well.   Sometimes, assorted concrete blocks can be found in the stream but a little footbridge would be most appreciated just here.

On the other side, shake the water (or whatever) off your bags and veer off to the right to find the small Bridleway-signed gate in the wire fence across your path. The field beyond this gate slopes up to fenced-in trees on your left whilst the River Crane flows along the tree line on your right.   Follow the grassy track up to a farm gate and a smaller gate next to it - also Bridleway-arrowed - and the field still slopes down from left to right as you ascend.   After the gate, there is a wire fence on your right as you ascend for about 1/4 mile.

At the top of the field, you emerge onto a wide entrance with a plethora of gates and a stile right next to the busy B3081.

Now, turn to Route 1 - Stage 1 for the return section of your walk.   Actually, you'll be sharing the return along the B3081 verge with the Route 1 walkers who left you at the Drove Road.

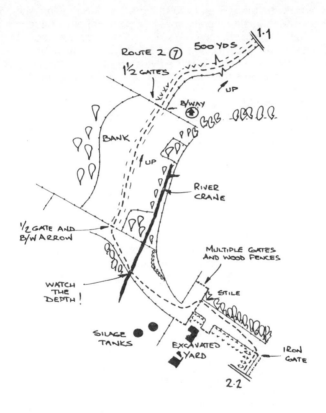

ROUTE 2 ⑦

1½ GATES

500 YDS

1·1

↑ UP

B/WAY

BANK

↑ UP

RIVER
CRANE

½ GATE AND
B/W ARROW

MULTIPLE GATES
AND WOOD FENCES

STILE

WATCH
THE
DEPTH !

SILAGE
TANKS

EXCAVATED
YARD

IRON
GATE

2·2

ROUTE 3 - STAGE 1

SQUIRRELS CORNER TO MONKTON UP WIMBORNE

From the parking area, turn down the track into the beech, chestnut and pine woods, away from the B3081 and passing through a half-gate. In a few yards, a pair of tracks face each other across your path, leading into 'Private' woods. You soon arrive in a wide, grassy clearing with a wire-fenced field over on your right with a farm gate at the nearest end and a couple of pine trees where the clearing narrows again into your track. There are no Bridleway signs along here but this farm track is free to use as a Bridleway - fear not.

This hedged, downward slope leads you round a couple of bends, with the bank high on your left and the field dropping away on your right, to an opening into the left field and a pair of holly bushes in a dip. The grass-centred track rises slightly and, after openings into two right fields, keeps descending with high fields on the left and a dip down into the fields on the right, past opposite field entrances, a high hedge on the left and more openings before a left bend.

This particular track should be kept in mind when you start the return trip on the Ackling Dyke in a few minutes time as there couldn't be a greater contrast in route-making than these two diverse ways - one constructed as a military, marching road and the other winding as it will across identical landscape but with no urgency. I know which feels more relaxing, even without the occurrence on the Ackling Dyke. Oh! I haven't told you about that yet, have I?

Anyway, you now have confirmation that this is a true Bridleway - two posts, one either side of the track, carry 'Bridleway' arrows on their far side. More openings on your left side lead into the high fields and a hedged track on your right descends to the barns and farmyard of Manor Farm, Monkton Up Wimborne. As you arrive, between young beeches in the high hedges on both sides of the track, at a T-junction, turn right onto the tarmac road which comes from Wimborne St Giles on your left. The River Allen runs through the meadow field facing you as you turn around the hedged and fenced garden of Manor Farm.

Manor Farm, Monkton Up Wimborne. Page 134

132

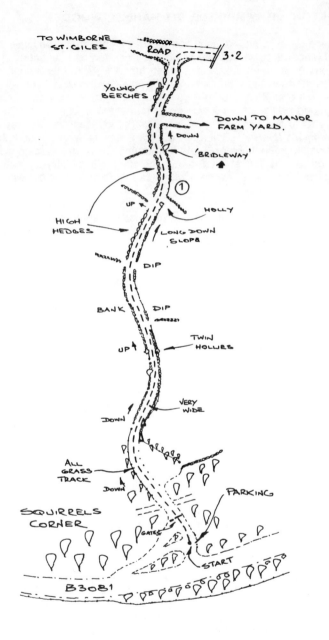

TO WIMBORNE
ST. GILES

ROAD

3·2

YOUNG
BEECHES

DOWN TO MANOR
FARM YARD.

DOWN

'BRIDLEWAY'

①

UP

HOLLY

HIGH
HEDGES

LONG DOWN
SLOPE

DIP

BANK

DIP

UP

TWIN
HOLLIES

VERY
WIDE

DOWN

ALL
GRASS
TRACK

DOWN

PARKING

SQUIRRELS
CORNER

GATES

START

B3081

133

ROUTE 3 - STAGE 2

MONKTON UP WIMBORNE TO HARLEY WOOD

The nice, level tarmac doesn't last long - on your route, anyway. Only as you pass Manor Farm, with its fine stone and flint chequered chimney breast, and the post box on the corner of the wooden fence. As the lane continues between hedges, turn left onto the much-used Bridleway (no signs) and, passing a farm gate into the field on your left, go through the cantilever gate across your path. *The young chalk-stream which flows under the bridge is the River Allen, just setting off to flow through some glorious meadowland all the way to Wimborne where it joins the River Stour.* The track is now raised on a hedged and fenced causeway to keep it clear of wet-weather flooding and, as a signposted Footpath goes off to your left at an S-bend, the track climbs steeply between banked hedges of beech and hawthorn with loose flints underfoot but with grass up the middle.

Nearing the top of the hill, there is an ancient yew tree on the right hand side. *After many fruitless enquiries into its origins, I can only assume that it was seeded by a bird many years ago.*

Then, at a wide opening on your left, you will see a recent plantation in the high field and there is another opening into the field on your right. You still have the young beeches growing in the high hedges as you reach a junction with the main track bearing round to the left. With a vast, wire-fenced field facing you, turn right instead onto a long, pebbly track. There are still no Footpath or Bridleway signs but this is a Bridleway. As you stroll along this track, high up on Harley Down, there are several specimen trees planted in the wide, double hedge on your right and the field on your left slopes away downhill. The fence soon becomes broken and interspersed with sparse hawthorns and, after a while, you will have fine views through the first opening in the right hedge to Pentridge Hill in the distance. If you intend to extend your walk after Route 3, you will have the conquest and exploration of Pentridge Hill in mind for later today.

Just past this opening, there was once a pile of cut logs on the right. It was here that I saw a stoat weaving in and out of the logpile. This isn't as irrelevant a statement as it may appear because stoats are the greatest enemy of rabbits and hares and their presence could greatly affect the prophecy of Armageddon which I mentioned some time ago.

But, before we come to that, just press on, past a couple more openings in the hedge on your right, past a Bridleway arrow (at last) by a track that goes off to your left, into a narrow strip of woodland known as 'Harley Wood'.

In these woods, another track turns off right but ignore it and keep straight on through to a crossing of Bridleways. *The embankments on the left and right are where the Roman Ackling Dyke has been cut through by the Bridleway and, just at the foot of the left bank, there is a memorial stone for John Ironmonger 1919-1986.* There are three Bridleway arrows on the far corner fence post.

Turn right onto the Bridleway between the Ackling Dyke and the woodland.

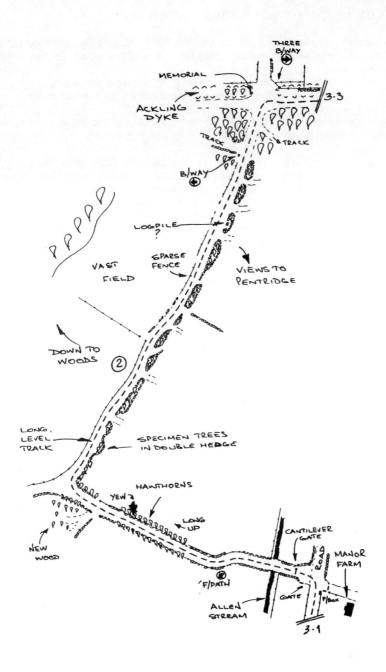

THREE
B/WAY

MEMORIAL

ACKLING
DYKE

3.3

TRACK

TRACK

B/WAY

LOGPILE
?

SPARSE
FENCE

VAST
FIELD

VIEWS TO
PENTRIDGE

DOWN TO
WOODS

②

LONG.
LEVEL
TRACK

SPECIMEN TREES
IN DOUBLE HEDGE

HAWTHORNS

YEW?

LONG
UP

CANTILEVER
GATE

ROAD

MANOR
FARM

NEW
WOOD

F/PATH

GATE

P/BOX

ALLEN
STREAM

3.1

135

ROUTE 3 - STAGE 3

HARLEY WOOD TO BOTTLEBUSH DOWN

Just before you follow the track up onto the top of Ackling Dyke, let me tell you why the stoat was so significant on Stage 2.   An old Dorset adage insists that,

*'When Cranborne is whoreless, Wimborne is poorless
and Harley Wood is hareless, the world will be at an end'*

It would be unethical to comment on the first part and too socially incorrect to comment on the second part, so I'll just worry about the hares.

Actually, there's more to worry about as you follow the path up to and along the top of the Dyke, with the woods down on your right and a fenced field down on your left.   *Some time ago, I walked alone down this part of the Roman Ackling Dyke, a route also used by Saxons and Normans and the scene of many localised disputes during the Bronze and Iron ages.   It was a warm, sunny and windless day and I was enjoying the shade from the overhanging trees. Suddenly, I felt a firm slap on my right shoulder as if somebody I knew had come up behind me.   When I turned round, there was nobody there.   Wondering what else could have struck my shoulder like that, I looked on the ground to see whether a broken branch had fallen - but there was nothing on the path.   I looked to make sure that I hadn't walked into a low branch - and there wasn't a low branch.   I still have no explanation for the slap on the shoulder but I don't like to conjecture too much.*

Anyway, continue your gentle, downhill stroll until you reach a clearing and the Dyke becomes flattened on its right flank.   After a Bridleway arrow, cross over the Monkton Up Wimborne road and continue straight on, with the Dyke submerged in trees on the left of the track.   The path is grassy and long but made difficult for walkers by the deep hoofprints hidden in the long grass.

The Dyke is now above head height as a track crosses your path and cuts straight through the Dyke into an open field beyond its banks.   *In this field, on Wyke Down, there are some fine Bronze age tumuli .*

Continue along the edge of the Dyke as the track soon widens, with the woods going away slightly to the right and with our path bending towards the Dyke after crossing another track which meets us from the right and goes over the Dyke into the tumuli field.   Bending left and right to follow the Dyke's path, the track now runs between the right wire fence and the Dyke but, after the first few yards, the grass tends to get a bit dense so go up onto the top of the Dyke where you will find a strangely carved stone and a thin path weaving its way between staggered hawthorns.   *Along the way, there are fine views from the top of the Dyke.*   After two cuttings through it, come down again at a clearing with two gates.

Now, for the final level stroll back to base camp, turn to Route 1 - Stage 2 and Route 1 - Stage 1 maps in that order.   You won't really need them because the way is so clear (and you'll be following them in reverse anyway because they're really 'departure' Stages for Routes 1 and 2).   However, the text does include a few observations which you may find interesting.

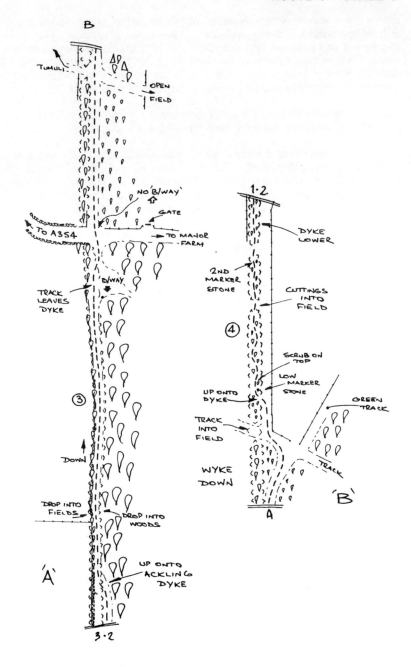

IN CONCLUSION

After such a breathtaking exploration of this beautiful county, where can I start with an appreciation of the splendours we have seen - or will see, if you're reading this before you even set foot outside? I didn't undertake these walks in the order in which they appear in the book and I don't expect that you will either. After each one, I thought that I must have seen the best that Dorset has to offer. Then I did another one and had the same thoughts all over again.

I have to confess that I got lost, or at least had a little difficulty in finding the right way, on several occasions but I didn't have this book to follow.

I tried to evaluate the best parts of all of these walks but, on reflection, it is really impossible to say categorically, 'This ridge walk with its superb views of the sea or vast, lonely downland was definitely the best' or 'That tiny church nestling in a sunny, bird song-filled valley was the most beautiful' or 'This or that fine country house in its magnificent park was the high spot of the walk'. However, if pressed, I would certainly choose the view from Swyre Head on The Encombe Encounter as embodying most of what Dorset is all about. From the ridge, the view encompasses fine, expansive coastal and cliff scenery, a pattern of farmland and a fine stone country house in the valley (with another one in the valley behind). There is a thatched village and a church in the distance and a folly on the cliff. At the same time, rooks argue in the woods, flocks of sheep quietly graze the fields and skylarks chatter above. It's a little bit of heaven.

Then again, Bottlebush Down and Pentridge Hill take some beating and I'm delighted to have found Melbury Sampford park and Chantmarle - and the lovely little churches of Melbury Bubb and Frome St Quintin. The villages of Ashmore and Compton Abbas were perfect focal points on an intriguing ramble through ancient woods and over high chalk downs with magnificent views. Spreadeagle Hill and Melbury and Fontmell Downs were brilliant, rivalling my original choice of Swyre Head.

And what can I say about Abbotsbury and the Gorwell Farm excursion? The ridge walk was wonderful and the dairy farm valley by The Grey Mare and Her Colts was so far removed from the popular village of Abbotsbury and St Catherine's Chapel hill as to feel strangely remote and peaceful whilst the ancient woods were, again, filled with bird song. The high ridge views of Chesil Beach, Portland and the coast to Devon were well worth the climb and the stroll near the sea, on the way to St Catherine's Chapel, was very pleasant indeed.

The walk from Wimborne Minster to Badbury Rings and the Kingston Lacy Drove around the beautiful National Trust park was fascinating and an easy introduction to these guided walks. For all that, my enduring memory of this particular excursion was the rich greenery with the huge old trees, the fine views from Badbury Rings and the lovely village green at Pamphill on the way back.

Of course, I'll have to leave you to make up your own minds, but don't do it until you've been on all of the walks.

BIBLIOGRAPHY

History and Antiquities of the County of Dorset: Rev John Hutchins 1861 - 64

Inventory of Historical Monuments in the County of Dorset: H.M.S.O. 1970

Dorset Churches: Sir Owen Morshead: Dorset Historic Churches Trust 1976

The Place Names of Dorset - Parts 2 and 3: A D Mills of the English Place Names
Society - Edited by K Cameron.

Dorset Barrows: Leslie Grinsell F S A

Portrait of Dorset: Ralph Wightman: Robert Hale

The Old Roads of Dorset: Ronald Good

Inside Dorset: Monica Hutchings 1964

Unknown Dorset: D Maxwell 1927

Geology Explained in Dorset: John W Perkins: David and Charles

Geology and Scenery in England and Wales: A E Truman: Pelican Books

Gardeners' Encyclopaedia of Plants and Flowers: Christopher Brickell: R H S

Ashmore - A History of the Parish with Index Registers 1651-1820: E W Watson
M.A. of the Society of St Andrew, Salisbury 1890

Cranborne Chase: Desmond Hawkins: Victor Gollancz 1980

A Chronicle of Cranborne and Cranborne Chase: T W Wake Smart 1841

Purbeck Shop: Eric Benfield: Ensign Publications

ACKNOWLEDGEMENTS

Thanks again to my wife Janet for listening to my wild theories about landscape
formation and then putting me straight on the geology.   Thanks for providing me
with some wonderful picnics for my diurnal meanderings and for coming with me
on some of the walks.   Thanks to my son Harvey for the tale of the Chantmarle
poacher and to my daughter Emma for joining me on a mountain bike journey
around Kingston Lacy for a final check of the maps.

Thanks to all the staff at Lansdowne Reference Library, Bournemouth who
frequently delved into the Dorset archives to retrieve some dusty tome or other.
Thanks to the Local Studies Librarian at Dorchester County Library for finding the
more ancient and remote items and finally, thanks to the Rights of Way Section
at County Hall for sorting out problems at Compton Abbas and the Evershot area.

CIRCULAR DORSET RAMBLES

INDEX

GREEN FIELDS BOOKS

13 Dalewood Avenue, Bear Cross, Bournemouth, Dorset, BH11 9NR

Publication list

THE NEW STOUR VALLEY PATH
0 9519376 7 7   £4.95   A glorious... 60 miles in 6 days guided walk from Christchurch to Stourhead with intricate maps, folk tales, drawings and historical detail.

THE CRANBORNE CHASE PATH
0 9519376 2 6   £4.95   A superb 76 miles in 6 days guided walk from Wimborne Minster to Salisbury Cathedral to Shaftesbury Abbey and back with intricate maps, drawings and finely observed detail.

THE BLACKMORE VALE PATH
0 9519376 3 4   £4.95   A splendid 71 miles in 6 days guided walk from Blandford Forum to Dorchester to Yeovil and Sherborne and back across the Blackmore Vale to Blandford with maps, sketches and fine detail.

RAMBLES FROM DORSET TOWNS
0 9519376 5 0   £4.95   More, longer circular walks all over the less crowded areas of Dorset.   Some coastal walks, others over downland, in woodlands and farming country.   Between 5 and 11.1/2 miles with historical details, drawings and intricate maps.

HILL WALKING IN DORSET
0 9530338 0 5   £4.95   Circular walks to 20 of Dorset's most beautiful 'peaks' which, when conquered, are the equivalent of three Scafell Pikes (without the crampons, ice-axes or bivvy bags).   Lovely country walking with stupendous views.

MORE CIRCULAR DORSET WALKS
0 9530338 3 X   **£5.95**   A series of circular walks, mostly within the 5 miles range.   Some coastal walks, some inland (but within sight of the sea) and others in deepest darkest Dorset.   All with the customary notes, commentary and finely detailed maps.

DEAD INTERESTING DORSET
0 9519376 6 9   £2.50   An anthology of Dorset church epitaphs and ecclesiastic engravings - some humorous, some illustrating Dorset's place in world events and some with connections to Dorset's literary giants.

IF ORDERING BY POST, PLEASE ADD £1.00 PER BOOK TOWARDS POST AND PACKING